TAJ MAHAL

WONDERS OF THE WORLD

....

TAJ MAHAL

GILES TILLOTSON

P

PROFILE BOOKS

First published in Great Britain in 2008 by
Profile Books Ltd
3A Exmouth House
Pine Street
Exmouth Market
London ECIR OJH
www.profilebooks.com

1 3 5 7 9 10 8 6 4 2

Typeset in Caslon by MacGuru Ltd
info@macguru.org.uk
Designed by Peter Campbell
Printed and bound in Great Britain by
Clays, Bungay, Suffolk

A CIP catalogue record for this book is available from the British Library.

ISBN 978 1 86197 890 5

The paper this book is printed on is certified by the © 1996 Forest Stewardship
Council A.C. (FSC). It is ancient-forest friendly. The printer holds FSC chain of
custody SGS-COC-2061

FSC
Mixed Sources
Product group from well-managed
forests and other controlled sources

Cert no. SGS-COC-2061
www.fsc.org
© 1996 Forest Stewardship Council

To Madhav and his grandfathers,
Michael Tillotson and Kulbhushan Kumar

Let those who scoff at overmuch enthusiasm
look at the Taj and thenceforward be dumb.
Rudyard Kipling

CONTENTS

INTRODUCTION: ORIENTATION

The Taj Mahal is the queen of architecture. Other buildings might be as famous, but no other is so consistently admired for a beauty that is seen as both feminine and regal. Many people feel that to class the Taj Mahal as architecture is a mistake: it is both too personal and too magnificent. But it is also something of a cliché: it attracts the attention of advertisers and satirists almost as often as it is invoked as a measure of the sublime and the marvellous. Most of us, inevitably, encounter it first through photographs. We therefore approach the original in awe and trepidation, with our expectations ready to be either shattered or fulfilled.

Preconceptions, responses … ideas about the Taj Mahal and the history that shapes them, form the subject of this book. We shall find that what you think about the Taj Mahal depends on who you are, where you came from, when and why. A Mughal court poet, an English Romantic traveller, a colonial administrator, an architectural historian and a couple on their honeymoon (to give just a few examples) start with very different perspectives and purposes. The enduring solid marble construction presents an illusion of stability. The familiar view of the pristine monument from the entrance gateway is the very image of permanence. But the thoughts it has inspired have always been varied and changing. All these competing interpretations, overtly or not, represent claims to some sort of ownership of the building. Silent and compliant, the Taj will be what you want it to be.

WAH TAJ!

To many people in India the name 'Taj Mahal' suggests not only a building but a blend of tea. The famous architectural wonder in Agra has lent its name to a popular blend that is a staple commodity in countless households. The packet bears an image of the building along with the catch-phrase that features in all its advertisements: 'Wah Taj!' A cry of admiration, 'Wah!' is traditionally uttered at Urdu poetry recitals, and so obliquely implies a further reference to the building by conjuring a world of Mughal sophistication and elegance. There is more than one irony in this claimed association. Taj Mahal tea is a decidedly mid-market product. Besides, tea was not produced in India until the nineteenth century. At the time the Taj was built the only source of tea was China. Its builders drank coffee.

But the use of the name goes beyond tea. Even amongst buildings there are numerous contenders for the title 'Taj Mahal'. Someone in Delhi uttering the phrase 'Let's meet at the Taj' would be inviting you to a 1970s tower block rather than suggesting an excursion to Agra. The building is one in a whole chain of Taj Group hotels that stretches across the country, following one of India's oldest and most famous luxury hotels: the Taj Mahal on the waterfront in Bombay (now Mumbai), designed in 1903 by W. Chambers and financed by the Parsee entrepreneur J. N. Tata, allegedly after he was refused entry to a Europeans-only establishment. Conspicuous in any image of the harbour, the Taj Mahal hotel has become one of Mumbai's iconic buildings and remains fashionable amongst connoisseurs of the high life. It has produced clones not just across India but from Sydney to San Francisco. These include some other landmark hotels, such as the Boston belle the Ritz Carlton, now renamed in honour of the Taj.

Of course, these and other such appropriations of the name imply a reference to the original. They stake a claim to excellence that works only by presupposing a familiarity with the source. They certainly spread the fame of the name. But they crowd the original round with a new constellation of meanings. In everyday speech the frequent use of the name 'Taj Mahal' to refer to tea, hotels and a host of other items ranging from packets of saffron to bars of soap, forms a mire that the contemporary Indian consciousness has to wade through to reach the Mughal building.

LOVE AND THE NATION

The Taj Mahal in Agra is a tomb. The most famous product of the Mughals, whose empire in India flourished between the sixteenth and eighteenth centuries, it enshrines the remains of the fifth emperor of the dynasty, Shah Jahan, and those of his second wife Arjumand Banu Begam, known as Mumtaz Mahal. She died before him, in 1631, and construction of the complex began almost immediately. Her grave is placed centrally within the building and that of Shah Jahan was added later, alongside. These and other circumstances have led to the conclusion that the tomb was intended, initially and primarily, for *her*; and this in turn has prompted the widespread interpretation of the building as a monument to love.

Here at least is one idea that is both international and historical: since the moment of its completion both Indians and foreigners have described the Taj Mahal as a symbol of love. This view is greatly assisted not only by Shah Jahan's known and documented affection for Mumtaz Mahal above all other women (a story that we shall return to) but also by the perceived beauty and perfection of the building itself. Few people in Mughal India (and no one since) could have gazed on the reportedly beautiful face of Mumtaz Mahal, but the building's beauty is taken as a metaphor for hers, and the place of burial is conflated with the buried. In this spirit, many commentators have described the building as 'feminine', and have seen it as expressing the patron's love, as if their own response to the anthropomorphised building must in some way echo the builder's feelings for the woman interred within. What else but passion, they ask, could have inspired something so perfect?

Entrenched in the popular imagination, this idea of the Taj as an expression of love has made it a favourite destination for honeymooners, who are likely to enact certain well-rehearsed rituals, notably having their photograph taken whilst seated on a marble bench with the monument as a backdrop. Such images are so widely circulated that Princess Diana only had to appear in this pose alone, on a royal tour of India shortly before the break-up of her marriage with Prince Charles, to convey to the world her sense of loneliness and loss. In fact, the bench has nothing to do either with the original design or with the love of Shah Jahan for Mumtaz Mahal: it was added only a century ago.

1. The Taj Mahal: the classic view from just inside the main, southern gate of the garden.

There have been sceptics. Those who oppose the 'symbol of love' theory appeal not to our sentimental but to our cynical side, not by denying the building's beauty but by insisting that it must have some explanation beyond the mere feeling of one individual for another. No one ever did anything so extravagant for love, they argue. We should be looking for some covert ideological agenda, or show how it was designed in the service of power. For example the American writer on Mughal India Wayne Begley appeals to our sense of reason by declaring that so grand a structure cannot be 'purely and simply' a tomb. On a different line of thought, the current leading expert on the building, Ebba Koch, hints that as a symbol of love it doesn't quite work for her, since its over-whelming beauty demands a passive response that is 'irri-tating to the adventurous'. We shall return to some of these alternative interpretations later in this book.

The Taj Mahal's secondary career has been as a symbol of India. The prize piece of India's heritage, it is seen to embody the country's celebrated history and civilisation. But by whom? Surprisingly, this idea is largely foreign in origin. In the eighteenth and nineteenth centuries it was eulogised more by Western than by Indian writers and artists. Ele-vated to the status of national symbol by outsiders, not until about 1900 was it accepted as such by Indians. Of course, Indians had long recognised its merits, but traditionally the architectural magnets for Indian travellers were more likely to be shrines: temples or the tombs of saints rather than of empresses. Early Indian visitors to the Taj, who came either as pilgrims or as sightseers, were far outnumbered by those going elsewhere. And this continues. Today the Taj is seen by nearly two million Indians per year. The Tirupati temple in southern India, meanwhile, welcomes nearly twelve million pilgrims per year. Yet it is the Taj that is recognised as the symbol of India. It is still seen as such abroad too; indeed, few outside the country will have heard of the Tirupati temple.

The other seeming oddity of the Taj's role as a national symbol is that it has achieved this status for Indians in spite of being Islamic. As Muslims, the Mughal emperors were members of a religious minority. In a country where the vast majority practise other faiths we might expect some resistance to a national symbol that could be associated with a period of Muslim dominance. Interestingly, by and large (excluding for the moment some lunatic fringes) no such association is made. The popular attitude towards it is secular rather than sectarian: it is regarded as common heritage rather than the legacy of one religious group. In a similar way, most Indians today would identify both the four-lion standard depicted on the country's currency and the wheel at the centre of the national flag as 'ancient Indian', rather than as 'Buddhist', though these symbols are of Buddhist origin. Few regard the buildings designed by Edwin Lutyens and Herbert Baker for the British imperial New Delhi as casting any shadow of colonial rule, for they are now better known for housing the country's president, parliamentarians and bureaucrats. Origins are not meanings, and in the popular mind the Taj is generically 'Indian'.

Sometimes this is stated overtly. The year 2005 was declared (with little historical accuracy) as the building's 350th anniversary, and in September of that year a crowd of people collectively offered at the building a shawl measuring 100 metres in length. Presenting a shawl to a person is a standard gesture of congratulation, but offering a shawl at a tomb is a religious rite in Islam. To avoid any misunderstanding, the members of this crowd were at pains to point out that they represented many different religions and that theirs was a 'secular shawl'. Reverence for the Taj was thereby removed from any specifically 'Islamic' context and a common ownership was declared.

UNORTHODOX TAJ

In playing down its religious associations, it may help that, viewed from an Islamic perspective, the Taj Mahal is itself unorthodox. Islamic law prohibits grand sepulchral architecture. Simple burials are preferred and ideally the grave should be covered with nothing but earth and bricks, to facilitate the raising of the dead on the Day of Judgement. Of the first six Mughal emperors (those traditionally called the Great Mughals), the first and the last, Babur (d. 1530) and Aurangzeb (d. 1707), insisted on adhering to this convention and have simple, open-air graves, respectively in Kabul and in Aurangabad. But there is often a tension between the demands of faith and the aspiration of rulers to commemorate themselves and their families. Historically, many Islamic regimes have built tombs regardless, and none more grandly than the Mughals.

More generally there is a *hadith* or religious tradition that records the Prophet's disapproval of any kind of ostentatious building, on the ground that it consumes too much of a man's wealth. The Mughals were aware of such ideas but they were also alert to the political and symbolic power of great architecture, and the tension was a matter of debate at court. The Emperor Akbar's companion and biographer Abul Fazl wrote:

'mighty fortresses have been raised, which protect the timid, frighten the rebellious and please the obedient. Delightful palaces and imposing towers have also been built; they afford excellent protection against cold and rain, provide for the comfort of the princesses of the harem, and are conducive to that dignity which is so necessary for worldly power.' So, expediency of various kinds won the day.

Some historians have suggested that the open doorways of Mughal tombs exempt them from the ban: not being enclosed, they are not really buildings at all but canopies over the graves. It is not clear whether this was also a Mughal argument, or, if so, whether anyone was persuaded: the Taj Mahal as a mere canopy seems a trifle far-fetched. Besides, the argument does not address the Islamic ban on delays in burial, and on the distant transportation of the body, both of which the builders of the Taj ignored.

A TAJ FOR ALL

No one, it seems, is willing to play by the rules. The original builders overlooked inconvenient aspects of orthodoxy, and modern devotees overlook unwanted historical associations, both in order to shape the Taj according to their own desires. In between there have been numerous efforts at recasting the Taj in different roles, and some outlandish interpretations. What are we to make of theories, soberly advanced, such as that it is merely one of a pair, whose twin was never built; that it is a gigantic symbol of the Day of Judgement; that it is not a Muslim tomb at all but an ancient Hindu temple; or that it is not really a specimen of Indian architecture, but Italian?

Suggestions like these will find a place in the chapters of

this book, not because they tell us much about the building itself (they do not) but because they are central to the 'Taj phenomenon'. Some of them stake claims of ownership, literal or metaphorical; others have been advanced with wider agendas about interpreting India's past; and together they keep the building in a state of flux. So this is only in part a book about the Taj of the Mughals: it is as much concerned with the building's career in Indian and Western imaginations.

Chapter 1 looks at the historical context and the human drama behind the building, particularly the relationship between Shah Jahan and Mumtaz Mahal. This aspect of the story has been as much contested as any other, with widely divergent accounts of their characters and motives – and serious discrepancies between the court histories and accounts by European residents in India at the time. The trick is deciding who to believe.

Unorthodox though it is, the Taj Mahal is by no means the only Islamic tomb in India. Chapter 2 considers its place in a larger pattern of tomb building, as well as explaining the secrets of its architectural success. This involves both tradition and innovation. Its design sustains and develops ideas that had been around for four hundred years and were to last for at least another hundred. Scattered across India are its many country cousins that are less well known, but which help to explain it. At the same time it was seen from the outset by both Mughal and foreign chroniclers as something exceptional, standing above the tradition from which it sprang. The frequent description of it as 'incomparable' may be misleading (to be pedantic, for there are many appropriate comparisons to be made) but it is also persistent. Almost every commentator has seen it as in some respect unique.

Although this cannot quite make it one of the original Seven Wonders of the World – an ancient list which could scarcely have included a seventeenth-century Indian tomb – many have sought its honorary inclusion, or have even ranked it higher. One of the first to do so was the French physician François Bernier, who was present in India at the time of the Taj's construction and averred: 'this monument deserves much more to be numbered among the wonders of the world than the pyramids of Egypt', which he described by comparison as 'unshapen masses and heaps of stone'. Somewhat less confrontationally, the eighteenth-century English diplomat Charles Malet called it 'deservedly the wonder of the *Eastern* world', a phrase that was echoed by the late-nineteenth-century local historian Syed Muhammad Latif. At the time of writing, the Taj has just achieved inclusion amongst the 'New Seven Wonders of the World', the subject of a world-wide popular internet vote organised by the Swiss adventurer Bernard Weber. The history of the building's reception, especially amongst foreigners – that is, the process by which it gained international recognition – is the main subject of Chapter 3.

Chapter 4 reflects on a different aspect of the building's reputation: its representation by artists, both Indian and Western, and references to it in later architecture. By this last I mean not only the continuing tradition of Mughal tomb building, but buildings of the nineteenth and twentieth centuries whose architects with varying shades of success have tried to invoke the Taj through visual resemblance. Unlike some other empires, the British Raj is not famous for its high aesthetic standards, but some of its later buildings ambitiously sought to emulate – or at least imitate – Mughal architecture.

A prime example is the Victoria Memorial in Calcutta, built in honour of a different empress.

This was also a period that saw a major restoration programme initiated by Britain's most controversial Viceroy of India, Lord Curzon. His efforts at the Taj Mahal have had a mixed reception. They are often judged to be largely benign, and they even received complimentary accolades from Jawaharlal Nehru. Postcolonial critics of the Raj have predictably been less willing to exonerate this exemplar of autocracy, and even his seemingly innocuous gift of a lamp has been minutely dissected for signs of colonial arrogance. It has been suggested that his understanding of Islamic art was based on little more than a boyhood reading of the *Arabian Nights*. Chapter 5 looks at these and other responses to what Curzon actually did at the Taj, and brings the story of its conservation up to date with some recent and ongoing disputes about its ownership, treatment and exploitation. There is a news item about the Taj in the Indian press almost every month: a remarkable circumstance that cannot be true of many comparable monuments elsewhere. These range from the claim to ownership of the building that was brought to court by a local Muslim charity board to the possible involvement of the chief minister of Uttar Pradesh (the state in which Agra lies) in sanctioning the now aborted plan to construct what can only be described as a shopping mall, linking the Taj with the Agra fort. Behind both these stories lie issues about conservation and care, and also issues of local interest groups who feel unfairly marginalised – issues which force us to ask how we might react if we had the Taj in our own home town.

Whatever else is contested about the Taj Mahal, there is no doubt that it occupies a place in the collective consciousness that stretches far beyond its Mughal origins. In India it has a record in product endorsement to rival both Amitabh Bachchan and Sachin Tendulkar, the country's leading film star and cricketer, respectively. Apart from tea and hotels, it has been invoked to promote everything from bath taps to life assurance. 'When it comes to building something permanent [a current company advises, over a picture of the Taj], whether it's your financial portfolio or a monument to love, patience has its rewards. Which is why investing in our long-term equity fund ...' A manufacturer of domestic paints, using the slogan 'Paint your Imagination', shows us the Taj remodelled in pink and blue. A dealer in shawls invites us to regard 'the Taj and the Pashmina' as comparable masterpieces, and suggests that his wares, though once designed for sultans, are just as well suited to 'the blue-blooded jet setters of today'.

In the summer of 2007 a huge model of the Taj was floated down the Thames in London to publicise a festival celebrating Britain's economic ties with India (see illustration 28, p. 164). No doubt it was thought that there could be no clearer or less ambiguous symbol. But the season also marked sixty years of India's independence, and in that context the images of the Taj sailing past St Paul's were suggestive of the expatriate or 'non-resident' Indian taking up rightful residence in the former imperial capital.

The commonest use of the name abroad is probably for Indian restaurants. There is no town in midland Britain without at least one Taj Mahal takeaway. Here the name is simply a recognisable sign of India, one that hints at a homogeneous or typical culture that does not in fact exist in India itself in any field – least of all cuisine, which is very regional. The average Taj Mahal restaurant serves up a version of India that is not quite foreign, but is concocted by émigrés to suit a foreign palate. The diners are not expected to be aware of fine distinctions, and the name 'Taj Mahal' does not necessarily carry a promise of serving *mughlai*, or Mughal dishes.

But then, one might ask, just how Mughal is the name 'Taj Mahal' anyway? It is usually said that the name derives from Mumtaz Mahal, the title given to the empress, which means 'select of the palace'. There is room for doubt about this: 'taj' need not be an abbreviation of 'mumtaz' since it is itself a perfectly good Persian word meaning 'crown'. It is also worth noting that the building is not called 'Taj Mahal' in the contemporary Mughal sources. Abdul Hamid Lahauri, the author of the *Padshahnama*, the official history of Shah Jahan's reign, calls it '*rauza-i munawwara*', meaning 'the illumined or illustrious tomb' (where *rauza* implies specifically a tomb in a garden).

It was François Bernier and other European observers who witnessed its construction who first called it the Taj Mahal. It seems unlikely that they invented the name: perhaps they picked it up from the residents of Agra. They called the empress 'Taj Mahal' too, which suggests they believed that the tomb was named after her. Their use of the name interchangeably for the woman and for the building began that conflation of the two that marks their history. In any case, it is to her and to her family that we must turn first, to tell the story of her tomb.

The scene of the tale is the city of Agra, on the banks

of the River Yamuna, a hundred miles or so to the south of Delhi. Amongst the largest and finest of the Mughal cities, it periodically served as their capital. It is less grand today, both decayed and redeveloped; but its skyline is still dominated by the shining dome of the building that everyone has come to see.

I

THE PLAYERS

Buildings that are strongly associated with individuals often seem to bear their mark. The shade of Henry VIII stalks the corridors of Hampton Court, and one feels that Ludwig II has only just stepped out of Schloss Neuschwanstein whilst the tourists take their round. The story of Mumtaz Mahal and Shah Jahan, of the devoted wife and the grieving husband, is so much a part of the mythology of the Taj that visiting the building feels almost like meeting a proxy. The Taj is a medium through which we encounter their personal relationship.

Tourist literature tempts us to read that relationship in terms of modern romantic passion. Most of us have a sense that love is a human constant, something that connects us with the remotest eras and cultures. But this particular love story was played out in the dangerous and conspiratorial world of an imperial court, and it all looks rather different when seen in that context. To begin with, the marriage was one in a series of alliances with the family of a Persian immigrant, who positioned themselves to exercise enormous influence over the court through three successive generations. Even by the standards of the Mughals, who had foreign origins them- selves, this family might have been regarded as rank outsiders

2. The interior of Itimad-ud-Daulah's tomb; watercolour on paper,
painted by Latif of Agra, *c.* 1820.

3. Cameo portrait of Shah Jahan; the work of an unidentified European
jeweller working in India, *c.* 1630.

in India; but ability, beauty, patience and luck brought them extraordinary prominence. The men served and the women married successive emperors, making their family indivisible from the imperial dynasty.

Visitors to Agra who allow themselves enough time to see what the tourist guides like to call the 'Baby Taj' – the tomb of Itimad-ud-Daulah on the other side of the river – begin to piece together fragments of this family saga, and draw in the characters who surround the Lady of the Taj. For Itimad-ud-Daulah was her immigrant grandfather; and his tomb was built by her scheming aunt, Nur Jahan, who was married to her frequently inebriated father-in-law, the Emperor Jahangir. The interconnected tale of these characters is the essential background to the building of the Taj.

MEETING THE FAMILY

Shah Jahan was born in January 1592. He was the third son of Jahangir, who was at that time the heir presumptive to the Mughal throne, being the eldest son of the Emperor Akbar (r. 1556–1605). The child's mother, one of Jahangir's senior wives, was a Rajput princess, the daughter of Raja Udai Singh of Jodhpur. It was Akbar who had adopted the practice of marrying women from India's established ruling families in order to cement his political allegiances with them. The Mughal empire claimed sovereignty over the territories of these rulers but in many cases allowed them considerable autonomy, to encourage them to accept Mughal power rather than resist it. Under Akbar the empire became a magnificent joint venture to which many contributed and from which many benefited, regardless of religious or ethnic differences. The

Rajputs were members of warrior clans who claimed descent (in many cases) from the Hindu god Ram, and could chart their ancestry (to the satisfaction of modern historians) at least to the seventh century. Rajput women who married into the imperial family were often given splendid Persian titles, but continued their own Hindu religious rites. Meanwhile their fathers and brothers, when they were not busy attending court, commanded the empire's armies and governed its provinces.

Jahangir was himself the product of Akbar's marriage with another Rajput princess, from Amber. This means that Shah Jahan, the fifth in line of a nominally foreign dynasty, was in fact three-quarters Indian: three of his four grandparents were Rajputs, descended from long lines of ruling families in Rajasthan. But this inheritance was not always apparent in Shah Jahan's outlook. Whilst his father had been generally open minded in matters of religious policy, and his grandfather had bordered on being a sceptic (and was indeed denounced by some as a heretic), Shah Jahan was a more orthodox Muslim. He drank very little, for example (despite his beautiful jade wine cup that is now in the Victoria & Albert Museum in London). He sustained the established alliances at a political level but did not himself marry any Hindu women.

In 1607 he was engaged to Arjumand Banu Begam (later given the title Mumtaz Mahal), who was the daughter of Asaf Khan, a prominent noble and the son of Itimad-ud-Daulah. As the betrothed couple were barely out of childhood, the marriage was not solemnised until 1612. In the meantime Shah Jahan had already married his first wife, a descendant of the Shah of Persia. A few years later he also married the daughter of another prominent Mughal courtier. The official historians do not disguise the political nature of the first and third alliances and it is only with hindsight that the marriage to Mumtaz is described in terms of special attachment.

Mumtaz's antecedents were not exceptional. Her grandfather – originally called Ghiyas Beg – had come from Persia in 1576. Despite being the son of a former governor of Isfahan, his career was not prospering and he felt he might fare better abroad. The obvious destination to choose was India, as the liberal court of Akbar was renowned for accommodating able foreigners who had something to offer. The Mughal court in fact viewed Persians with some ambivalence. Suspicious of them as Shias (since the Mughals themselves were Sunnis), and inclined to think they gave themselves superior airs, the Mughals nevertheless respected Persians as the inheritors of a long and rich artistic and literary culture.

The journey was not an easy one as Ghiyas Beg travelled along a caravan route with a pregnant wife and three children. They headed for Fatehpur Sikri, Akbar's temporary imperial capital situated some twenty-five miles to the west of Agra. Here Ghiyas Beg managed to get an introduction to Akbar and was soon given a position as revenue minister in Kabul (a city that at this time lay within the domains of the Mughal empire). His career amongst the Mughals was launched. Skilfully negotiating the turbulence of Mughal politics, he was rewarded at the start of Jahangir's reign in 1605 with a more prominent position at court, and his grandiose title Itimad-ud-Daulah, meaning 'pillar of the state'. And then his granddaughter was betrothed to the new emperor's son.

In the same year as that betrothal, Itimad-ud-Daulah's young widowed daughter (who was also of course Mumtaz's aunt) came to live at court. What a consolation it must have been to her in her bereavement to live so close to her parents, her elder brother Asaf Khan and her niece. Four years later, in 1611, she strengthened her family's ties with the imperial dynasty by marrying Jahangir. She became his eighteenth, and last, wife. So, even before the marriage between Shah Jahan and Mumtaz had been solemnised, the bride's aunt had married the groom's father. Jahangir gave her the title Nur Jahan, meaning 'light of the world', to echo his own name. How she came to this position and what she did with it is important to the story of Mumtaz and justifies a digression.

When Itimad-ud-Daulah had set out from Persia, the future Nur Jahan was the unborn child in his wife's womb. Their daughter was born on the journey, at Kandahar, and was originally named Mihr-un-Nisa. Commentators on the family's history have tended to play up the hardships of the road, suggesting that at one point they were robbed of all they possessed; that they had only two mules between them; that the distraught parents had to abandon the newborn infant by the side of the road, convinced that they could not care for her; and that they were reunited with her only because she was rescued by the merchant in charge of the caravan, who by chance selected her own parents as the most suitable guardians for the foundling. All of this might be true: it has certainly been widely believed and often repeated. But it might equally be an embellishment added to enhance the 'rags-to-riches' element of the family saga.

Mihr-un-Nisa grew up with an awareness of her Shia and

4. The Rajput Bride: an idealised image of Indian royal women,
by William Daniell, engraved 1835.

Persian heritage. In 1594, at the age of seventeen, she was married to another Persian wanderer, Sher Afgan (the 'lion slayer'), who had fled the Persian court on the assassination of the Safavid ruler Shah Ismail II in 1578, and had found service in India under the Mughal commander Abdur Rahim Khankhanan. Such a marriage, between one imperial servant and the daughter of another, would have been arranged by the families and approved by the emperor.

The last few years of Akbar's reign, however, were dangerous times. The emperor had turned sixty and people were on the lookout for signs of his ailing. His son Jahangir, now in his thirties, was impatient to assume control; so much so that he set up a rival court in Allahabad, minted coin in his own name and styled himself 'sultan'. He need not really have worried. His father had a forgiving temperament even when faced with revolt; and Jahangir's most likely rivals, his two younger brothers, were both busily engaged in drinking themselves to death – which indeed they soon achieved. Jahangir's main impediment was his own drinking habit. Many who were close to the emperor regarded the imperial prince as unstable and unfit to rule, and promoted the idea of bypassing Jahangir in favour of his own teenage son Khusrau. Their counter rebellion seemed to have Akbar's covert support.

Choosing which side to be on in such a situation was fraught with danger. For some it was impossible. Khusrau's mother, who was also of course one of Jahangir's wives, besides being the sister of one of Akbar's most trusted generals, was so appalled by the lot of them that she took a lethal overdose of opium. Mihr-un-Nisa's husband, Sher Afgan, despite having earlier served Jahangir, chose to be loyal to Akbar, the serving emperor, thus taking a gamble on the future.

By the time that Akbar died in October 1605, Jahangir had been reconciled with his father and he was duly proclaimed emperor in succession. Sher Afgan was forgiven in an ambiguous sort of way: he was put in charge of a small landholding in distant Bengal, both a promotion and a punishment posting. But his troubles returned early in 1607 with renewed stirrings of the Khusrau rebellion, as some of those who had lost out (but survived) thought it was worth another try. Jahangir, though engaged in the conquest of Kandahar at the opposite end of the empire, nevertheless had time to wonder whether Sher Afgan was implicated in this fresh disloyalty and sent the governor of Bengal to find out. Taken by surprise, Sher Afgan treated this visit as an accusation, and being a hot-blooded type ran his sword through his inquisitor before he could open his mouth. He was immediately cut to pieces by members of the governor's guard.

The widowed Mihr-un-Nisa, who had just turned thirty, was ordered back to court in Agra where she was given as a lady-in-waiting to one of Akbar's dowagers. This was in fact a privileged position which did not reflect the disgrace of her late husband. Her appointment is one of a number of instances of a Mughal emperor displaying compassion towards those innocently caught up in a feud that was not of their making. It was especially generous since, at this time, Mihr-un-Nisa's father, Itimad-ud-Daulah, was temporarily under a cloud, facing a charge of embezzlement.

So things continued for four long years; and then the wheel of fortune turned again. It was the custom at the Mughal court to celebrate the Nauroz or Persian New Year – a pre-Islamic festival, which carried no religious significance to the Mughals, but was a good excuse for a party. A standard part of the jollity involved the women of the imperial palace setting up a bazaar within the zenana (the women's apartments), where female traders could offer them their wares and they would shop at stalls, as if in a normal market. Being within the zenana, the women could go about unveiled. The only man who was permitted to watch the fun was the emperor. This was the light-hearted but somewhat charged context in which Jahangir first encountered Mihr-un-Nisa, face to face, in the spring of 1611. He was evidently much taken with her. Two months later he married her.

THE FACTION

As empress, Nur Jahan was quickly to become the dominant influence on Jahangir, eclipsing other wives, just as her father and brother, Itimad-ud-Daulah and Asaf Khan, were promoted over rival courtiers. These three Persian immigrants – father, son and daughter – became the most powerful faction at court. And it was a threesome more than a foursome because Jahangir, though nominally at the centre of the family group, became increasingly willing to leave decision-making in matters of state to them whilst he had another drink. Much of the administration of the Mughal empire, and especially of the court, lay increasingly in their hands.

The story as told so far can be attested from reliable contemporary sources, including official court histories and Jahangir's own memoirs. There are alternative versions of the tale, some later in date and some concocted even during the lifetime of the protagonists. This was inevitable. Given Jahangir's rapid transition to a state of utter dependence on Nur Jahan, the cynics and the gossips put their heads together in the bazaars and began to question whether perhaps these two had known each other for longer than they admitted. Perhaps their famous love affair had a prehistory. Perhaps they met even before she was married to Sher Afgan. Perhaps she was married off to Sher Afgan just to separate the lovers. Perhaps Jahangir had had Sher Afgan killed to get him out of the way (there was something distinctly shady about the way that poor man died) and then brought her back for his own purposes. Or perhaps the whole design was not Jahangir's but *hers*: she had been scheming to entrap the emperor with her beauty and her demure smiles, so as to advance herself and her family.

All of this and more has been proffered by a variety of commentators, both Indian and foreign. Some of the early versions were no doubt prompted by the frustration felt by men such as the English ambassador to the Mughal court, Sir Thomas Roe, who found it impossible to transact the business they hoped for because Jahangir's responses had always been prepared in advance by Nur Jahan, to whom they had no access. Other versions equally obviously were inspired by the desire to make an already good story even better. They are still frequently repeated and believed by tourist guides and their audiences. But they all come up against the same immovable objection: how to account for the four-year interval between Nur Jahan's return to Agra and her marriage to Jahangir. If they had known each other earlier and were impatient to be reunited, why would they lie low for four years?

Whether it was achieved wholly by scheming or partly by chance, the power of the faction became a reality. It was further strengthened in 1612, when the formalisation of the marriage between Asaf Khan's daughter Mumtaz and Shah

Jahan widened its membership. With two elder brothers, Shah Jahan was not the legitimate heir, but he was demonstrably the ablest and most ambitious of the princes, his father's favourite and the most likely successor. Nur Jahan supported his cause. To do so, she had to overcome a scruple. Shah Jahan's mother – the Jodhpur princess Jagat Gosaini – was one of the emperor's most senior wives and potentially a rival for his attention. To advance Shah Jahan was by implication to advance Jagat Gosaini. But as Nur Jahan had no children of her own by Jahangir she was going to have to support someone else's son eventually, and Shah Jahan had the advantage, as well as being the most likely winner, of being married to her niece. So she cultivated the prince and ensured that he assimilated her own family's values and outlook.

The authority of the faction endured for a decade. No business could be effected, no preferment procured, except through them. And with the next generation already involved and ready to take over, things must have looked hopeless to those on the outside, who did not enjoy their favour.

But then the cracks appeared. The first blow was the death in 1622 of Itimad-ud-Daulah. His wife, Nur Jahan's mother, had died the year before, and as Jahangir himself recorded in his memoirs, his father-in-law simply gave up the will to live. Nur Jahan was distraught at the double loss, and commissioned the construction of an exquisite and elegant tomb for them, in their garden on the bank of the River Yamuna. A glistening casket of decorated white marble, its design – in ways that will be explored in a later chapter – prefigures that of the Taj Mahal.

With Itimad-ud-Daulah gone, there could be no rallying of the faction's surviving members because the other threat came from within. Shah Jahan enjoyed early success in his military career, and his stature grew with age and with each fresh conquest. Meanwhile Jahangir was visibly succumbing to drug addiction and to alcoholism, and Nur Jahan belatedly realised that her own power depended on her position as empress, that is to say on her husband remaining alive. An able successor such as Shah Jahan, once he had taken over, would have no further use for her. Her place of influence, at the emperor's ear, would be taken by her niece. Having earlier assiduously promoted her remarkable stepson, she now switched allegiance to a younger, less outstanding prince named Shahriyar, who would have greater need of her should he make it to the throne. From her first marriage, with Sher Afgan, she had a daughter named Ladli Begam, whom she now arranged to be married to Shahriyar, to bolster his claim. This was the third intermarriage between the imperial family and the descendants of Itimad-ud-Daulah; but it was designed to divide the family bonds, not to augment them.

The pawns were not up to the game and the manoeuvre failed, not least because Nur Jahan's brother Asaf Khan was bound to continue supporting his own daughter and son-in-law. When Jahangir died at the end of 1627, Shah Jahan duly succeeded to the throne, dispatching Shahriyar and some other superfluous male relatives along the way. Nur Jahan was sent into a quiet retirement in Lahore, and India found it had a new empress: Mumtaz Mahal.

SHAH JAHAN AND MUMTAZ MAHAL

Shah Jahan's comparative orthodoxy in religious matters is generally recognised as a mark of the early influence on him of Nur Jahan and other members of Itimad-ud-Daulah's family. It lasted into his maturity but he did not seek to impose his views on the next generation. His eldest and favourite son, Dara Shikoh (born 1615), was something of a mystic in the manner of Akbar; he translated Hindu scriptures, whose message he considered entirely consistent with the Qur'an, and dreamt of achieving 'a confluence of the two oceans'. Dara Shikoh was to be declared an unbeliever by his more orthodox younger brother Aurangzeb (born 1618), whose loud professions of piety were to cause their father much disquiet.

These two brothers were both sons of Mumtaz Mahal. Indeed, Mumtaz, was the mother of all of Shah Jahan's surviving children, with the exception of one daughter. She gave birth to a total of fourteen children – eight sons (of whom four died in infancy or early childhood) and six daughters (of whom three died young). The fourteen pregnancies covered a span of just eighteen years. This record is often cited as evidence of the degree of Shah Jahan's attention to her, which credible contemporary accounts confirm. His historian Inayat Khan commented that 'his whole delight was centred on this illustrious lady, to such an extent that he did not feel towards the others [i.e. his other wives] one-thousandth part of the affection that he did for her'. It is clear that Shah Jahan was as devoted to Mumtaz as his father had been to her aunt, though more productively and without the abject dependency. That Mumtaz was influential, no one doubted, but she was not the manipulative puller of strings behind the veil of purdah. She has been seen rather more as the support and comfort of her warrior husband.

For Shah Jahan's career, both as a prince and as emperor, up until the early 1630s, was primarily a military one. The length of the list of his successful campaigns cannot be attributed entirely to luck or to able lieutenants: he must at the very least have had the leadership qualities that made those under his command exceed their own expectations. From early on he accepted tasks that others had deemed impossible, subduing parts of the Deccan and defeating the forces of the Rana of Udaipur, the last and most recalcitrant of the Rajput chiefs.

One might wonder how he managed to combine this active service in the field with such a prodigiously fecund home life. The answer – shocking in modern terms – is that when he went on campaign he took Mumtaz with him. Her pregnancies were not only unrelenting, they were often endured in camp conditions. It was in just such a situation, in Burhanpur in 1631, that Mumtaz died, shortly after giving birth to the fourteenth child, a daughter named Gauhar Ara. She was thirty-eight.

The tradition that the exhausted Mumtaz, sensing that her end was near, implored her husband to build her a worthy tomb and to have no further offspring, is fictitious, inspired in hindsight by his building of the Taj Mahal and his failure to marry again, though it is hard to believe that a man in his position stayed celibate for the remaining thirty-five years of his life. The tradition, recorded by the nineteenth-century historian Muhammad Latif, that the dying Mumtaz 'looked on the king with despair and tears in her eyes, and admonished him to take good care of her children and her own aged father and mother when she was herself no more' is more credible, though also not attested.

On the other hand, there is good evidence from the more sober contemporary histories that Shah Jahan's grief at this loss was genuine, profound and long. For a week he refused to see any noble or adviser or to conduct any state business – a serious omission for someone with his responsibilities. He did not observe the normal daily custom of appearing at a balcony to show himself to the people. For as long as the army remained based in Burhanpur he visited his wife's temporary grave every Friday to recite the *fatiha*, the prayer for the departed. Islam requires from the believer full trust in the will of God, against which too overt a display of sorrow on bereavement might be considered an infringement. Shah Jahan was said to remark that but for this, and for his sense of duty to the empire, he would have preferred to abdicate and divide power among his sons. In fact from this time onwards he did take a less active role especially in military campaigns, leaving command of the imperial forces to his sons (who were in any case beginning to come of age), whilst he remained at the capital. Not that this gave him much solace. Whenever he visited Mumtaz's former apartments in the palace he could not stop himself from bursting into tears. For two years he forswore the wearing of jewellery or perfume and refused to listen to any music. And as the portraits show, his beard went white.

Almost as soon as he got back to Agra he selected a site on the bank of the Yamuna for her permanent resting place. The owner of the land, the Raja of Amber, was compensated with other properties in the city. Six months after her death, Mumtaz's remains were brought from Burhanpur to Agra by Shah Shuja (her second son), and were reburied on the site. The construction of the tomb over her grave was to take another twelve years; and the time, the effort, the cost and the splendid result have all been taken as further evidence of the power of Shah Jahan's grief.

Towards the end of 1657, Shah Jahan fell ill. The events that followed bear directly on our understanding of the Taj. Some writers have believed that Shah Jahan's own burial alongside Mumtaz within the Taj, rather than in a separate mausoleum, was brought about by what happened next.

Shah Jahan was at this time in Delhi, which he had re-established as the capital ten years earlier. Throughout the 1640s he had been engaged on his largest and most ambitious building project: the laying out of an entire new city of Delhi, to be named Shahjahanabad after himself, and situated on the west bank of the Yamuna to the north of the older settlements. The imperial apartments in the fortified palace that overlooked the river are his greatest achievement in residential architecture and formed the setting for a daily routine of unparalleled dignity and opulence in the later years of his reign.

With the onset of illness he was content to leave the administration in the hands of his eldest son and presumed heir, Dara Shikoh, and retire to his earlier palace in the fort in Agra to recuperate. His three other surviving sons were serving in the distant corners of the empire. Shah Shuja was in Bengal, in the east; Murad Bakhsh in Gujarat to the west; and Aurangzeb was in the Deccan, in the southern part of central India. Each harboured ambitions to succeed to the throne. Each sensed that this illness spelt the end, and became fearful that Dara's position at the centre would work to his advantage, as indeed their father had intended. So each now declared himself emperor, collected his army and prepared to march on Delhi, to take the throne by force.

Shuja moved first, early in 1658, and so had to face the main body of the central imperial army, dispatched from

5. Shah Jahan and leading courtiers survey wedding gifts
(displayed on the floor) presented to the imperial prince Dara Shikoh
(top left, with Aurangzeb). Painting by Balchand, *c.* 1635.

Delhi by Dara under the command of one of his sons. Shuja was repelled but escaped back to Bengal, where he awaited another chance. Meanwhile Aurangzeb sensibly proposed an alliance with Murad against their common enemy Dara. The duo twice succeeded in breaking through against the remaining central forces that were sent against them, the second time under Dara's personal command. Dara was forced to flee back to Delhi without an army, whilst the combined forces of Aurangzeb and Murad surrounded Agra.

Up until this point all three rebel brothers stoutly maintained that their only concern was to visit their sick father, to be assured with their own eyes that he was on the path to recovery. Their goal was not Delhi, they said – of course not – but the infirmary in Agra. Why they needed to drag armies with them on such compassionate visits was not explained. In response, their father sat up in bed and declared that he was feeling fine now, thanks, and they were welcome to call at their convenience – an invitation which Aurangzeb and Murad, now sitting outside and laying siege to the Agra fort, declined to take up. Historians have further accused Aurangzeb of dissimulating about his ultimate intentions, suggesting that he told Murad that his ambition was to become a hermit, and that he was only helping to save the empire from the atheist Dara. The story is convincing in so far as it plays on Aurangzeb's reputation for being both pious and duplicitous; but one must wonder whether such a ruse would have persuaded any of his brothers.

In any event, the alliance and the pretence did not last long, as Aurangzeb found means to imprison Murad. Shortly afterwards he captured the Agra fort and sent in his son to confine Shah Jahan under house arrest. There could be no going back from this point. Aurangzeb could not appear before his father in any guise but that of rebel and usurper, so he refused to meet him altogether. He left his son in charge of the imperial prisoner and spent the next few months chasing Dara and Shuja around the empire in a game of cat and mouse. Shuja was again pushed back into Bengal, and then abruptly and mysteriously disappeared. What happened to him has never been ascertained, though he was last seen in an area of the Bengal coast that was notorious for pirates.

The French physician François Bernier and the Venetian adventurer and quack Niccolao Manucci were both, at different times, caught up in the camp of the fugitive Dara, and each has left vivid impressions of his state of desperation. Bernier recalls how at one point the exhausted party was refused entry into the city of Ahmedabad by a governor who was too afraid to offer sanctuary:

> *The shrieks of the females drew tears from every eye. We were all overwhelmed with confusion and dismay, gazing in speechless horror at each other, at a loss what plan to recommend, and ignorant of the fate which perhaps awaited us from hour to hour. We observed Dara stepping out, more dead than alive, speaking now to one, then to another; stopping and consulting even the commonest soldier.*

Dara considered fleeing to Persia, but he was too slow to put this plan into effect. He was captured and sent to Delhi, where Aurangzeb had him put to death; he was buried in the tomb of Humayun (the second Mughal emperor). Murad, after being transferred from one prison to another, was also eventually executed. Indeed the purging extended to the next generation with the confinement and poisoning of Dara's eldest son.

The principal survivor of the carnage was Shah Jahan himself, as even Aurangzeb could not stoop to patricide. This was not because the deposed emperor still enjoyed strong popular or influential support. On the contrary, there was soon no one to speak for him. Bernier remarked, 'I can indeed scarcely repress my indignation when I reflect that there was not a single movement, nor even a voice heard, on behalf of the aged and injured monarch', as those whom he had elevated soon transferred their allegiance to the new authority. But whilst Aurangzeb could find excuses for killing his brothers – Dara, after all, was an atheist and Murad was himself guilty of murder – he could not kill his father without tarnishing his image as a holy and humble servant of God.

So Shah Jahan was kept in confinement in Agra, and this situation continued for eight years, until his death in 1666. During this period father and son never met, and their relations – conducted through letters – were not cordial. Shah Jahan was permitted every personal luxury apart from his liberty, but he was not always treated with respect by his guards and his complaints to Aurangzeb were often ignored. He could exact revenge only in petty ways, such as refusing to surrender some jewels that Aurangzeb had demanded.

This long twilight of Shah Jahan's life, spent in elegant imprisonment in the gorgeous pavilions of the Agra palace, with his eldest daughter Jahanara as his chief companion and solace, has inspired much myth-making. We are to imagine the aged Shah Jahan reclining lazily in a balcony whilst gazing wistfully across the bend in the river towards the Taj Mahal, filling his final days with reflections on happier times. This

6. The private apartments of Shah Jahan in the Agra fort; built by him in the 1630s and the scene of his imprisonment in the 1660s.

image was fixed in the popular mind by a work of 1902 by the artist of the Bengal Renaissance, Abanindranath Tagore.

Others paint a different picture. Manucci (who had a nasty mind) imagined Shah Jahan engaged in endless sexual self-indulgence, and alleged that the illness of 1657 that sparked all the trouble, and the final illness that killed him, were both urinary infections brought on by the over-use of aphrodisiacs. Even the sober Bernier reported rumours that Shah Jahan was guilty of incest with Jahanara, and that he had persuaded a handily daft mullah to give a legal opinion in justification of the practice, on the ground that a man should not be denied the fruit of his own tree. The enduring and more popular perception casts Jahanara in the role of the dutiful and faithful daughter, the foil to her cunning and deceitful younger sister Roshanara, who was the favourite of – no prizes for guessing – brother Aurangzeb.

It was certainly Jahanara who took charge of matters when her father died. She informed the commander of the fort and summoned both the city *qazi* and a *syed* (legal and religious authorities) to perform the funeral rites. As retold by the nineteenth-century writer Muhammad Latif, the former emperor's body was taken from the pavilion in the palace known as the Saman Burj and

> removed to the hall close by, where it was washed according to the form prescribed by Muhammadan law. The body having then been enclosed in a coffin, holy passages were read over it. Finally the body was placed in a chest or receptacle of sandalwood, and the coffin, followed by a procession of mourners, was conveyed out of the fort through the low gate of the tower, which used to remain closed, but was opened for the occasion ... Hoshdar Khan,

viceroy of Agra, accompanied by officers of state, reached the bank of the river at day-break, and the coffin, having been conveyed across the river, was interred with due formalities, by the side of the tomb of Mumtaz Zamani, in the mausoleum built in her honour by the deceased emperor, who was now following her to the grave.

In spite of the viceroy and his officers, and the retinue of mourners, there is something quiet, almost hushed, in this account of a dawn embarkation, of an emperor's final passage to another world.

Aurangzeb, in Delhi, is reported to have wept on hearing the news of his father's death. According to Latif again, he told his nobles that it had been his earnest desire to be present during his father's last moments, to meet him face to face for the last time, to receive his blessings and to participate in the funeral, but, alas, all this was denied him. Latif says that 'the courtiers and nobles who were present were shocked'; and well they might be by such an outrageous display of crocodile tears.

Aurangzeb went further. He paid a visit to Agra, to weep again over the graves of his parents and to read the *fatiha*, the prayer for the souls of the departed. He visited Jahanara in the fort, to comfort her and offer his condolences. And then he decided to prolong his stay in Agra so that he could repeat both actions. He visited the Taj every day, read the *fatiha*, and distributed alms to the poor; and he then went to call on Jahanara, and advised his nobles to send her their own messages of greeting. The famous gem-studded Peacock Throne – a magnificent object commissioned by Shah Jahan and synonymous with his reign – was ordered to be brought down from Delhi and installed in the spacious Hall of Public Audience in the fort, in preparation for a pompous durbar held during the festival of Eid, when Aurangzeb presented himself enthroned to the assembled multitude.

All of this begins to look less like grief and more like an occupation, addressed to the city of Agra. For the last eight years the citizens of Agra at least were aware that the empire had two emperors: the one in Delhi and the one incarcerated in their midst. The usurper had favoured Delhi, but with the father now safely out of the way, he had come to parade about as a public benefactor and to sit on his purloined throne. Nothing could have made more explicit the passing of an era. Shah Jahan was truly dead and buried.

Aurangzeb continued to live and rule for a further forty years. His power was never again seriously threatened or challenged, but he remained neurotic and untrusting. He was especially wary of his senior Rajput nobles and thus undermined the principle of co-operation on which Akbar had constructed the empire's foundations. In hindsight historians consider Aurangzeb's very longevity as one of the early forces that first began to weaken the structure of the empire, which had seemed at its strongest and most splendid during the era of Shah Jahan.

THE JEWELLED DAGGER

From summarised narratives like this, the splendour of the Mughal empire might not always be apparent. It was a ruthless world. Dara Shikoh, humanist, aesthete and poet, but also imperial prince and aspirant, suffered the most barbaric public humiliation before he was put to death. Khusrau, the prince whom many considered better suited to rule than his inebriated father, was blinded on Jahangir's orders, and later killed by Shah Jahan. Even a more sedentary career like that of Itimad-ud-Daulah had its anxious moments, when he was out of favour or was outmanoeuvred by a jealous rival. No one emerges from the tale without blemish, and everyone suffered as a result of the fears and vices of the others. It is not that they were simply all immoral, or lacking in compassion. The story also shows them to be capable of the normal bonds of affection, and even of passion. But they lived in constant fear of betrayal or being overpowered, and this made them rash (like Sher Afgan) when challenged, and unforgiving in victory. Such vulnerability to forces outside one's control or even influence must have made them feel at times very much like pieces on a chess board.

This atmosphere is well captured in one of the most famous of all Indian films, *Mughal-e-Azam* (1960). The Taj and its story have featured in numerous Bollywood movies, some more successful than others. *Mughal-e-Azam*, the most popular cinematic portrayal of the Mughal world, in fact centres on a slightly earlier period, spinning out a (somewhat misunderstood) episode involving an alleged early love affair of Jahangir's, during the reign of Akbar. The fact that the sets anachronistically reflect the later architecture of Shah Jahan's court is a gift to the pedantic critic and shows how – in the popular mind – 'Mughal' means the era of the Taj. The film's story suggests this too, as it is a tale of tragic love, which explores the conflicts between personal bonds and imperial politics.

In real life, even as they plotted to assassinate each other, the Mughal princes and ministers patronised and consumed

7. A Mughal knife and dagger, with scabbards,
decorated with jewels and enamel work.

some of the finest works of art the world has ever seen. These include the textiles and jewellery with which they adorned themselves, the portfolios of paintings and illustrated manuscripts that they kept in their libraries, the music they listened to, their vessels and utensils of everyday use and the buildings – the palaces, mosques and tombs – where they lived, prayed and were buried. They knew it was good. They were not simply fortunate in the artists and architects who served them, they were patrons who were worthy of those they employed. As foreign commentators at the court privately conceded, Jahangir's connoisseurship of paintings and Shah Jahan's knowledge of gems outclassed the professionals in their respective fields.

The visual culture of the Mughals, so distinctive and instantly recognisable, was not conjured out of nothing. Its success was the product of the skilful blending together of the many different traditions that were available to the artists to draw on, including the Mughals' own central Asian heritage and the expertise and many long-established styles of India itself. The empire's greatest legacy is perhaps this composite culture; and that culture's most outstanding masterpiece is the building to which we now turn.

2

....

THE DESIGN

The design of the Taj Mahal has been mythologised as much as the couple it enshrines. Writers from the past, and scholars and controversialists of more recent times, have offered competing definitions of its style and divergent accounts of how it was all achieved. Modern popular accounts, by contrast, tend to avoid discussion of the architecture itself. Journalists always use the defining epithet 'symbol of love', never 'Indo-Islamic' or any other term which might point to its design. Your tourist guide might tell you that the design is based on Humayun's tomb in Delhi (partly true) and that once it was finished the architect's hands were chopped off to prevent him repeating the feat (quite untrue). But beyond this meagre information the building's style is left to speak for itself. As visitors we might not even notice the omission. Forewarned about its appearance from countless images, we are apt to take its style for granted.

But architectural designs do not spring out of nowhere. The remarkable achievement of the Taj lies in its manner of combining various traditions, and part of its meaning comes from the connections it makes. Before addressing the myths surrounding the design, it is worth examining what these connections were.

The designers of the Taj Mahal drew inspiration from three related traditions: the architecture of the Mughals' central Asian homeland; the buildings erected by earlier Muslim rulers of India, especially in the Delhi region; and the much older architectural expertise of India itself.

The founder of the Mughal dynasty, Babur, inherited a small kingdom called Fergana, in present-day Uzbekistan. The victim of various rivals and misfortunes in early life, he was unable to hold on either to this inheritance or to the city he most aspired to control, Samarkand. He revered Samarkand as the capital of his ancestor Timur, the late-fourteenth-century wandering affliction also known as Tamburlaine (and the inspiration of a famous play by Christopher Marlowe). For Babur, Timur was not just an unstoppable conqueror; he had also been a patron of all the most civilised arts, including architecture. Amongst his military achievements, Timur had visited Delhi in 1398, sacked it, and replaced the tottering Tughluq regime with one of his own choosing before sweeping out again. It was this precedent that suggested to Babur, over a century later, the idea of turning his attention to India. His defeat of the ruling Sultan of Delhi, Ibrahim Lodi, at the battle of Panipat in 1526 launched Babur on a new career and provided him with a new home.

But neither Babur nor his successors ever forgot where they had come from and they remained proud of the legacy of Timur. They were also descended from Chengiz Khan, the Mongol, a relationship reflected in the name Mughal. But it was the Timurid heritage that they were most proud of, to the point of obsession. Apart from the many inscriptions in which they had themselves referred to as members of the house of Timur, this sense of identity is well captured by a fragmentary painting (now in the British Museum) depicting some of the Mughal emperors seated with the sons of Timur at a sort of grand imperial garden party. The event shown is a historical impossibility as it combines people from widely separated periods of time. But the obvious purpose of the painting was to depict not an event but an idea, an association that was deeply embedded in the Mughals' sense of self. Timur was the ancestor of choice.

This Timurid identity is also reflected in some of the Mughals' most conspicuous buildings. One obvious example is the tomb of Humayun, the second Mughal emperor, built in Delhi in the 1560s, early in the reign of his son Akbar. More than a memorial to an individual, this building was a declaration of permanence on the part of the whole dynasty, and indeed it became the burial place for many future members of the imperial family. Yet it speaks of their foreign origins, as the lines of its domes and of its recessed arches evoke the architecture of the lost city of Samarkand. This imagery was to be carried forward to a later and similar project, the Taj Mahal.

To explain the second source of inspiration – the architecture of Islamic India before the Mughals – we have to go further back in time.

Islam came into India through two routes. One was maritime, mercantile and peaceful; the other was overland and violent. The ports of India's western coast, from Gujarat down to Kerala, had been connected with trade in the Arabian Sea since Roman times. Islam arrived by this route when some of the Arab traders converted in the seventh century, and those of them who settled were integrated into local communities as another new element in an already heterogeneous mix. Those who came overland from the north-west, by contrast, had no intentions to trade or even, initially, to settle. From the start of the eleventh century, warlords ruling areas in present-day Afghanistan began to make excursions across the mountains of the Hindu Kush, to sack India's wealthy temple cities and carry the loot back home. Their presence became permanent only from the end of the twelfth century, when a confederation of Rajput clans which had come together in an effort to stop them was defeated, and Muhammad of Ghur found himself unexpectedly in control of Delhi.

He too went home (he couldn't stand the climate), but he left behind a deputy. By 1206 this deputy had declared himself independent of his masters and was ruling a sizeable area around Delhi in his own name. This was a new political entity, generally now known as the Delhi sultanate. In the course of the next three hundred years (up until the Mughal conquest) this sultanate expanded from its Delhi base; but it also occasionally fragmented as the governors appointed from Delhi to administer provinces at the remote corners took advantage of the distance to establish their autonomy over new, regional sultanates. The ruling regimes were often dislodged either by internal revolt or through a fresh wave of foreign invasion, with power passing usually to another Muslim group. By the beginning of the sixteenth century large areas of north India, all the way down as far as the Deccan, were under Muslim rule of one kind or another, but it was disunited.

Against this background the Mughal conquest of 1526 could be seen as little more than another phase of competition for the largest and most central of the Indian sultanates. Not apparent at first was the manner in which the Mughals would manage to re-conquer the provinces and unite them into a vast empire. In doing so they acquired territories that had been under Muslim rule for three hundred years or more, and had an equally long history of Islamic architecture. The earlier sultans, whether central or provincial, had built forts and palaces, mosques and tombs, madrasas and caravanserais. All this amounted to a formidable building stock, a firm foundation of precedents on which the Mughals could construct buildings of their own.

Armies on the move rarely include architects amongst their personnel. They more often have specialists in blowing up than in constructing buildings. Timur had a reputation for sending to Samarkand all the architects of distant places that he graced with a visit; but that entailed a movement of architects out of, not into, the conquered domains. The conqueror who settles and wishes to build has to rely on local expertise. He will recruit the professionals who are close at hand.

In India they were available in abundance. India had a tradition of stone architecture dating back to the third century BC. The earliest examples were excavated or rock-cut; the later examples employed post-and-beam construction. Good building stone was plentiful (a circumstance which at once distinguishes India from the deserts of west and central Asia) and so was the knowledge of how to work it. The great temples built for Rajput kings at sites like Khajuraho, Gwalior and Osian reveal an extraordinary level of skill in stone-carving, and the tradition that they represent still flourished. This material and the expertise that went with it were to form the third essential resource for the Mughal designers.

Of course, these main sources of inspiration – Timurid, sultanate and Indian – are by no means as clearly divisible

[49]

as I have implied. Timurid and sultanate architecture have strong common ties with Islamic architecture elsewhere, particularly in Persia; and sultanate architects had been reliant on Indian expertise long before the arrival of the Mughals. It was not simply three discrete traditions but a grand melting pot including these and others that the Mughals had to draw on. Nevertheless, it is clear that the Mughals themselves had a sense of these three points of reference, which they could still distinguish amidst all the cultural cross-currents. In choosing the essential forms and plans, they followed the precedents set by earlier Muslim rulers in India; to highlight their distinctive origins they attempted on occasions to give their designs something of a Timurid inflection; and they deliberately engaged with local expertise and skills in the process. These three sources are each important in trying to understand how the Taj's design works.

THE TOMB'S FORM

Task: the emperor requires a tomb for his empress. How do you go about designing a tomb in Islamic India? What will it look like? There is no regional or indigenous precedent to assist you at this level, because the Hindus don't bury their dead; they cremate them and disperse the ashes. But there are plenty of earlier Muslim tombs in India that might offer some suggestions.

When India's first Muslim conquerors faced this problem they had to look abroad for an answer. Despite the orthodox preference for simple burials, early Islamic regimes had developed a variety of impressive tomb types. The most straightforward is a single square chamber surrounding the grave,

8. Hathi Pol or Elephant Gate at the entrance to Gwalior fort, built *c.* 1500; one of the few specimens of pre-Mughal Indian architecture that was admired by Emperor Babur.

9. The tomb of Ghiyas ud-Din Tughluq (d. 1320) in Delhi.

topped by a dome and entered through an arched doorway. The architectural volume is as simple as it could possibly be – a big box with a raised lid and a hole in the side – though of course the surfaces could be lavishly embellished with decorative brickwork or coloured tiles. We can find a precedent of this type in the tomb of Ismail the Samanid (d. 943) in Bukhara. This was the form used for the burial of the early Delhi sultans, such as Iltutmish (d. 1236) and Ghiyas ud-Din Tughluq (d. 1320). The chief difference is that where the Bukharan and other foreign models are made of brick, the Delhi tombs are of stone, simply because stone was available in Delhi and so were the stonecutters. It does make a difference, though. Iltutmish's tomb has a stunningly rich interior with intricate carving over every inch. Ghiyas ud-Din's tomb is more restrained with respect to detail but strikingly incorporates stones of two colours, with white marble set off against red sandstone.

The body, in both these cases and in all later ones, is interred on a north–south axis, with the head at the north, so that the face can be turned sideways, or westwards, to face towards Mecca. The west side of the building is closed, to incorporate a *mihrab*, a niche like those in mosques which indicate the *qibla* or direction of Mecca. The other three sides can be open, but one should be encouraged to enter from the south, at the feet of the buried person.

An early variant on this simple plan was to make the building octagonal rather than square. An octagon inevitably alludes to the primary building of Islam, the seventh-century Dome of the Rock in Jerusalem, which marks the spot from which the Prophet made his ascent into heaven. A building which is sometimes described as the first monumental

Muslim tomb – the Qubbat al Sulaybiyah in Samarra (c. 862) – has a similar octagonal form. This variant was introduced into the Indian subcontinent in the fourteenth century, starting with the magnificent tile-clad tomb of the saint Rukn-i-Alam in Multan (c. 1320).

In some later Indian examples, the plan is slightly more elaborate, with a veranda surrounding the central octagonal chamber: a sort of lean-to gallery that envelops the building. This pattern was adopted for the tombs of the fifteenth-century Sayyid sultans of Delhi (the dynasty set up by Timur), and also by some of their successors in the early sixteenth century. It was revived again during the period 1540–55, when Humayun was dislodged from the throne and went into temporary exile. A nobleman of the period built himself a tomb of this form in Delhi and the usurper who had defeated Humayun, Sher Shah Sur, built more elaborate multi-tiered versions for his father and for himself in Sasaram in Bihar. The form made its final appearance in the tomb of the Mughal noble Adham Khan, built in Delhi in the 1560s, that is two hundred years after its first introduction.

One is bound to ask, what is the veranda for? A covered but open-sided space, a veranda is normally an extension to the living area of a house, a mid-zone between interior and exterior that provides shelter and airiness at the same time. It is still today a common feature of Indian domestic architecture. So what purpose does it serve in a house for the dead? An obvious answer is that it would facilitate the movement of visitors walking around the tomb. Such an action is a gesture of reverence. Babur, for example, records in his memoirs visiting and circumambulating the tombs of saints, and the later Mughals did the same.

Tombs of saints are one thing. Pilgrims visit the tombs of Sufi saints and circumambulate them whilst praying for intercession, for a boon. But the practice conveys something slightly different in the cases of sultans and nobles. A prayer offered at the tomb of a sultan can only be intended for the benefit of the dead man's soul. It is a prayer *for*, not *to*, the departed. This explains why, despite the exceptions mentioned above, the majority of tombs for political figures do not have a veranda, and most adopt the simpler, square arrangement.

Even so, there was a tendency over time to construct tombs that were ever larger and more elaborate, as the expression of grandeur has its own inflation. A great leap forward came with the building of Humayun's tomb in Delhi in the 1560s. Standing on a vaulted terrace that is over three hundred feet wide, it is enormously larger and grander than any previous tomb in India. Its arrangement is an ingenious combination and elaboration of both the square and octagonal types. The central octagonal hall containing the sarcophagus is surrounded by lesser halls of the same shape, linked by a network of corridors. All of this is contained within outer walls that would be square but for the chamfering, or slicing of the corners, which makes an irregular octagon. The exterior volume (excluding the dome) looks like a rough cube composed of five interlocking octagonal blocks.

In scale and structural complexity, Humayun's tomb puts all precedents into the shade. Mughal sources attribute it to a Persian architect named Mirak Mirza Ghiyas, who was specially recruited for the purpose. But whilst much was new and dependent on imported expertise, there were also continuities. All earlier tombs in India might be overshadowed but they have not been altogether forgotten. The basic principles

10. Humayun's tomb, Delhi; as seen by an artist of that city *c.* 1820.

are unchanged. Humayun's tomb is still in essence a big box with a raised lid; its geometry is founded on the square and the octagon; and it is recognisably a descendant of the tomb of Ghiyas ud-Din Tughluq, built in the same city over three hundred years earlier.

Those same principles, as developed in Humayun's tomb, were the starting point for the designers of the Taj Mahal. The plan and volumes are actually somewhat simpler. Or, one might say, neater. The development is not so much a further elaboration as a refinement of the design. Whilst the integration of the octagonal blocks is left visible on the exterior of Humayun's tomb, in the Taj Mahal they are pushed into the same line to create more unified façades. In place of the arches of various sizes, there are now just two sizes, with the central arches being twice the height of the flanking ones; and the chamfering is precisely calibrated to match the corners with the flanking arches and thus create a sense of movement or flow around the building.

The scale has increased again. The width of each side is 30 feet more than in Humayun's tomb, and the total height, including the finial above and the podium below, has soared to 240 feet. More important than mere size are the improved proportions. Without the finial and podium, the building's height is the same as its width, so that its extremities form a cube. Everything is held in perfect equilibrium. Considered apart, Humayun's tomb is majestic enough, but by comparison with the Taj it looks a trifle ungainly: it lacks that clarity in the relation of parts that makes the design seem inevitable.

The internal organisation of the Taj is somewhat simplified too. There is the same central octagonal hall, with lesser halls of the same shape surrounding it at the corners, but

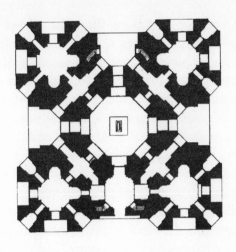

11. The ground floor plans of Humayun's tomb (above)
and the Taj Mahal (below).

the linking corridors run along the main axes of the building itself rather than at angles of 45 degrees, and they form a
sort of internal circumambulatory passage. In addition to the
four corner octagonal halls, there are four rectangular ones
between them. The plan is therefore a variant of the type
known as *hasht bihisht* (literally 'eight paradises'), a term that
describes a radial symmetrical grouping around a double-
height centre. This plan, though clear enough when drawn, is
not of course immediately apparent to the visitor. But we are
given some hint of it even from the exterior by the grouping
of the domes. The enormous central dome, placed over a high
drum, is surrounded by four smaller domes over octagonal
pavilions. This pattern also has its source in Humayun's tomb,
though the corner pavilions and domes are there much less
pronounced. A frequent component of Indo-Muslim tombs
since the fifteenth century, such domed pavilions, known as
chhatris (literally, 'umbrellas'), are ultimately of Indian origin,
and are common in early Rajput forts, for example. Like the
veranda, the *chhatri* is a local form that had been assimilated
into the generic vocabulary.

So, the 'massing' of the Taj Mahal – the arrangement of
the basic architectural volumes – does not involve a single
idea that had not been tried in India before. And yet it combines and refines established ideas in ways that make them
seem wholly spontaneous and original.

THE TERRACE

Before looking more closely at the surfaces of the Taj and
their ornamentation, let us broaden the perspective to consider its setting. For, as almost every commentator on the Taj

has pointed out, much of its glory depends on its placement amongst satellite buildings and in a garden.

The tomb is surrounded, first of all, by the four minarets which occupy the corners of the podium. The use of white marble as the sole surface material for all three components – tomb, minarets and podium – encourages us to read them as a unity. In one sense this is odd. A minaret is a tower from which the muezzin announces the time of prayer; as such it is a standard feature of a mosque but forms no functional part of a tomb. Even one of them would be superfluous here; four are positively gratuitous. The only thing approaching a precedent is the arrangement of four minaret-like towers over the gateway in front of Akbar's tomb at Sikandra (1605–12). There, as at the Taj, they are purely ornamental.

From time to time people have measured the minarets, and they assure us that they lean slightly outwards. A favoured theory to explain this is that they were deliberately built in this way so that if they fell in an earthquake they would not strike and damage the tomb. A more likely explanation is that they have to lean outwards in order to appear straight, to correct the optical illusion known as parallax. If they were completely straight then viewed from the ground they would appear to converge towards the central dome. Neither of these sensible explanations is sufficient to prevent periodic scare stories in the Indian press. Each time a journalist (on holiday perhaps) learns the intriguing fact that the minarets tilt, a story appears under the headline 'Monumental Neglect', warning that they are on the point of collapse like the Tower of Pisa. The Archaeological Survey of India, the government body that is responsible for the maintenance of the Taj, periodically has to reassure the country's ever-vigilant Supreme Court that the minarets are stable.

The marble podium which supports both tomb and minarets stands in the centre of a much larger terrace of red sandstone. Though rising only a few feet above the level of the garden, this terrace nevertheless gives the group an extra elevation to make it more clearly visible from a distance, and also accommodates two further buildings.

On the west side stands a mosque. Unlike minarets, a mosque may often be included as an adjunct to a tomb. Sometimes the relationship is reversed. The tomb of the early Delhi sultan Iltutmish was built in the precincts of the great mosque known as the Quwwat-ul Islam, as was the smaller tomb of one of the mosque's later *imams*. Another early-Mughal-period *imam* and poet, best remembered by his pen-name 'Jamali', built his tomb in a compound adjoining the mosque where he preached. In such cases the tomb is sited at a pre-existing mosque in order to benefit from its sanctity. Elsewhere, the mosque is conceived as part of the tomb complex, to provide a prayer hall for those who visit the tomb for religious purposes. That is the purpose of the mosque at the Taj, and indeed it is still regularly used for the Friday prayer, the only time when the complex is freely and exclusively accessible to Muslims and its religious identity is asserted. It is an elegant building of red sandstone, designed to complement without unduly distracting attention from the tomb.

At the opposite end of the terrace stands its mirror image, a second building that replicates the form of the mosque. Oriented the wrong way, this cannot be used for prayer. People facing it would have their backs towards Mecca, and the building accordingly lacks the *mihrabs* or niches that normally indicate the proper alignment for worship. It is often called the Mihman Khana ('guest house') and is described as an assembly hall for the temporary accommodation of those who attended the annual Urs, or commemoration of Mumtaz on the anniversary of her death. These events were certainly regular features of the early life of the complex. But the explanation has the air of an attempt to find a better rationalisation than the obvious one. For the main purpose of this building is to balance the mosque: it is a compositional device that maintains the overall symmetry of the design, a function that is reflected in its more popular epithet, Jawab, meaning 'answer'. It is as extravagant as the minarets, and equally successful in furnishing the tomb with a suitably magnificent setting.

THE GARDEN

Broadening the frame still further, the whole terrace occupies merely one end of an enormous garden. Much more than mere landscaping, the garden contributes crucially to the tomb's design, its meaning and even initially to its economic life.

Divided into quarters by streams of water that bisect it and meet at a pool in the centre, and surrounded by a high wall, the garden follows a long-established form known as a *char bagh* (literally, 'four gardens'). This form is of pre-Islamic ancient Persian origin. It was developed for a hostile terrain, where everything outside the enclosing walls is desert and everything within is fertile and fruitful. It creates a space apart, a defiance of the environment. In Islamic Persia this idea was further developed to turn the garden into a symbol of paradise. Indeed the word 'paradise' conflates the symbol with the symbolised since it originally referred to the wall surrounding a garden of this form.

The Qur'an frequently mentions a garden as the reward awaiting the faithful. The image of the afterlife it presents involves endless leisure in a walled garden or enclosed vineyard, with fruit trees, pavilions built over water courses, gushing fountains, cushions to recline against and a plentiful supply of wine. The wine is not the only beverage, but it is certainly there: 'A picture of the Paradise which is promised to the God-fearing! Therein are rivers of water which corrupt not; rivers of milk whose taste changeth not; and rivers of wine, delicious to those who quaff it' (Sura 47). The wine explains why the garden includes a vineyard; and we should note that this heavenly garden, though conducive to relaxation, is also productive, and not merely ornamental.

In Islamic cultures the terrestrial 'paradise' garden becomes a representation of the heavenly. The rivers tend to be of water, and they are more for irrigation than for drinking; but the garden's form, its fecundity and its promise of recreation were understood as aspiring references to the afterlife described in the Qur'an.

This idea was slow to be introduced into India. The early Delhi sultans seem not to have adopted it, though with gardens being so vulnerable to decay it is hard to establish this with certainty. Soon after the Mughal conquest, Babur confided to his diary a list of India's shortcomings, including the alleged absence of walled gardens. In a much quoted passage he grumbles that, amongst other deficiencies, there are 'no grapes, musk melons or good fruits; no ice or cold water; no good bread or cooked food in the bazaars; no hot baths; no colleges; no candles, torches or candlesticks'. Of course it was all an exaggeration, and partly intended for literary effect. India had in abundance everything that he said it lacked, but not in forms that he was ready to recognise. Gardens in particular had been an important component of palace architecture in India for over a thousand years; but they were not laid out on the cross-axial plan. They were not *char baghs*.

So Babur claims the distinction of introducing the *char bagh* into India. The claim may be disputed, but he certainly built a number of them throughout his newly acquired territories; and in some places, such as Agra, it was the first thing he did, even before building a mosque. One of the first that he built was in Dholpur in Rajasthan. Known about from a reference in his diary, this had disappeared from view but was rediscovered in 1978 by the American scholar – and author of the most informative and readable book on Mughal gardens – Elizabeth Moynihan.

More likely to have been a Mughal innovation, despite the simplicity of the idea, was the combining of the *char bagh* garden plan with funerary architecture. This combination almost suggests itself: if the *char bagh* is understood as an image of paradise, what better setting could there be for a tomb? And there were further reasons for combining them. A place developed as a garden during a patron's lifetime might later prove to be the most suitable or readily available site for his tomb. The tomb built by Nur Jahan for her parents stands in a garden that had previously belonged to them and which Jahangir refers to in his memoirs as Itimad-ud-Daulah's 'residence on the riverbank'. Nobles tended to build tombs during their lifetime (perhaps unsure whether anyone else

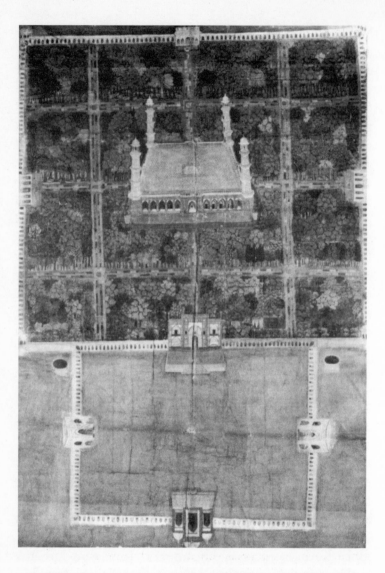

12. Jahangir's tomb, Lahore; gouache on cloth, by an artist of Lahore, late eighteenth century.

would bother once they were gone) and then used them in the interim as garden pavilions; and this practice established further associations between gardens and tomb architecture.

Under the patronage of the emperors this association was worked out on a monumental scale. The first in a series of variations on the theme was Humayun's tomb in Delhi, set in a vast *char bagh*, where each of the four quarters is divided by additional water channels into eight equal parts. And the pattern is further developed in the gardens of Akbar's tomb at Sikandra, built in the early years of Jahangir's reign, and of Jahangir's own tomb at Lahore, built under the patronage of Nur Jahan from 1627. The garden of the Taj is therefore the fourth in a sequence. Measuring 1,000 feet on each side, it is also the largest and the most complex in plan, with each of the quarters being divided (by paths rather than additional water channels) into four, and then into four again, creating a total of sixty-four square plots. In the earlier three cases the tomb was placed in the centre of the *char bagh*. The Taj is removed to an adjacent terrace. Besides responding to the riverside site, this arrangement allows the plan of the garden to be clearer: the basin at the crossing of the two rivers is restored to the centre, and so the paradise imagery is more emphatically asserted.

This imagery does more than provide an appropriate setting for a tomb, it changes the building's meaning. Each of the garden's component parts responds to the Qur'anic description. How then does one assimilate a vast building into this scheme? The current leading authority on the Taj, Ebba Koch, has persuasively argued that we are to see it as a representation of the heavenly mansion of the deceased, as a depiction of Mumtaz's abode in heaven. Such an edifice is certainly part of the Qur'anic vision: 'Life in this world is but a play and pastime; and better surely for men of godly fear will be the future mansion! Will ye not then comprehend?' (Sura 6). The twentieth-century American artist William Congdon intuitively got it right when he remarked of the Taj, 'It is not terrestrial architecture, but heavenly architecture.' Many other commentators have been tempted to see it as something sent by heaven rather than built by mortals – an idea that its mortal builders almost certainly intended them to have.

The importance of the garden to the meanings of the whole complex is one reason to be unhappy with its condition today. Its present care does not begin to approach the highest horticultural standards, and the layout reflects a well-intentioned but unscholarly attempted restoration of the early twentieth century. To be fair to that attempt, gardens in general are so changeable that it is often impossible to get an accurate sense of what a particular garden looked like in earlier times. But we can get some idea about the Mughals' gardens – and why they were different from what we now see at the Taj – from their literature and paintings.

First of all, Mughal gardens, like the Qur'anic heaven, were productive. Fruits that are mentioned as having been grown in them include apple, apricot, cherry, mango, mulberry, peach, pear, plum, pineapple, banana, guava, pomegranate, quince, melon and watermelon. To this list we must add many varieties of citrus fruits – lemon, lime and orange – besides dates, figs, grapes and sugar-cane. Nuts that were cultivated include almond, walnut and coconut. How many of these were originally grown in the garden of the Taj we cannot now be sure, but we do know that the fruit from the trees was a source of income that paid the wages and pensions of the tomb's attendants, the *khadims*.

The Taj had other sources of income, too. It owned land, as the emperor endowed it with a number of villages from which it could generate revenue like any other landlord. The purpose-built shops and caravanserais in the area adjoining the tomb complex to the south – an area once known as Mumtazabad but now called Taj Ganj – also provided much-needed income to maintain both the building and its staff. The shops generated 200,000 rupees a year according to Muhammad Latif. It is unlikely that the garden yielded as much, but certain that it played some role in the economic life of the tomb complex. By the nineteenth century the carefully planned economic support system had broken down, but even then the trees within the garden were let out to local gardeners for a fee.

The other feature of the garden that is important when we try to imagine its original form is the riverside setting. As tourists, like members of the public in Mughal times, we approach the garden from the south, from the land side, after crossing the outer courtyard and passing through the garden's magnificent entrance gate. Shah Jahan, by contrast, arrived by water (not just when he was in his coffin, but when he was alive). He selected the site because of its proximity to the river.

There are other surviving fragments of Mughal gardens dotting the riverbank at various places, including the garden tomb of Itimad-ud-Daulah and the well-known Ram Bagh (more correctly Aram Bagh or 'garden of peace'), traditionally associated with Babur but which in its present form dates from the reign of Jahangir. These few remains were once parts of a continuous chain of gardens, lining the riverbank on both sides without interruption throughout the length of the city. Most of them have entirely disappeared, but using an eighteenth-century map that was made for the city's governor, Ebba Koch has been able to reconstruct the original pattern of their distribution and ownership. The emperor and his women, the imperial princes and the leading nobles of the court, each had their own garden, facing the river and accessible from it. In time, as their owners died, many of them became tomb sites, like the garden of the Chini ka Rauza, the tomb of the finance minister Afzal Khan (d. 1639), situated a little upstream from Itimad-ud-Daulah's tomb.

This context explains the placement of the Taj. At one level, it is just another riverside garden with a tomb, standing towards the end of the line because it was built later than many of the others. The difference lies not in the idea but in the scale of its execution. The garden of the Taj completely overshadows its neighbours. And the stroke of genius was the placing of the tomb not in the centre of the garden but on a terrace over the riverbank, thus making it visible from every other garden through the length and breadth of the river.

BLACK TAJ AND MOONSHINE

One of the most persistent myths about the Taj Mahal is that it represents only half of the intended scheme. As if what is there is not enough, the story is often told that Shah Jahan originally intended to build a separate tomb for himself, a replica of the Taj in black marble, facing it from the opposite bank of the river, and linked to it by a bridge.

The source of this idea is an assertion made by Jean-

Baptiste Tavernier, a French jeweller who visited India to trade in diamonds on several occasions between 1640 and 1667. In his travelogue, published almost a decade after his return, Tavernier comments, 'Shah Jahan began to build his own tomb on the other side of the river, but the war with his sons interrupted his plan, and Aurangzeb, who reigns at present, is not disposed to complete it.' This sounds like a simple statement of what could have been common knowledge at the time, furnished as it is with circumstantial detail about the Mughal civil war, and a comment on Aurangzeb's notorious parsimony towards his father. One might observe that he makes no mention of the bridge, nor of the colour black, nor of it being a replica (these being embellishments added by later spinners of the yarn), but the basic element – the second tomb for himself – is in place.

The honest truth is that we have no way of knowing what Shah Jahan's private intentions were, or even if they remained consistent between his commissioning of the Taj in 1631 and his loss of freedom to act in 1658. There is no record of him expressing a preference either for a separate tomb or to share his wife's. His burial, as we have seen, was managed by his most trusted daughter, but whether its manner coincided with what he would have most wished for, we cannot know.

What we can know for sure is that Tavernier's claim finds no corroboration from any other contemporary source, either Indian or foreign. Yet it has been very widely believed. English travellers in the late eighteenth and early nineteenth centuries repeated it as a matter of fact. Muhammad Latif, the author of a scholarly study of Agra published in 1896, tells it in a manner that is obviously derived from Tavernier, pinning the blame for the abortion of the plan on Shah Jahan's

13. Percy Brown's 'conjectural realisation' of the two-Taj scheme,
from his *Indian Architecture: Islamic Period* (Bombay, 1942).

imprisonment and the 'austere' Aurangzeb. Percy Brown, a colonial arts administrator who in 1942 published a standard work on Indian architecture that is still widely read, describes the theory as 'well established' and presents his readers with a conjectural drawing of how the completed scheme might have looked.

Others too have argued in its favour. For evidence beyond Tavernier they have tended to point to some ruins on the opposite bank – a bit of wall and a half-collapsed tower – that are said to have been part of the abandoned project. Or they have noted the arrangement of the graves inside the Taj, with Mumtaz occupying the central place and Shah Jahan added asymmetrically to one side, surely an indication that his burial here was an afterthought, they say.

The latter circumstance (as many others have pointed out) is not the mystery it is presented as. Mumtaz lies in the centre because she died first. The same arrangement is found in the tomb of Itimad-ud-Daulah, where the body of his wife, who predeceased him, is placed centrally. The ruins on the opposite bank were, perhaps, a little more suggestive. Until 1995–7, that is, when the area was excavated by an Indo-US collaboration in a project directed by Elizabeth Moynihan. They found the remains of a garden, of the same dimensions as the garden of the Taj, and perfectly aligned with it. Scholars were previously aware of a couple of references in Mughal sources to a garden called the Mahtab Bagh (or 'moonlight garden'), across the river from the Taj; and now – behold – here it is. Not another Taj, but a lost garden. The old wall and the tower were part of its perimeter, not the foundations of another tomb.

Seasonal fluctuations and the occasional drift of the

shallow-bedded river had obviously caused much erosion to this as to many of the other gardens along its banks, and the Mahtab Bagh had almost entirely disappeared. It survived at least until 1789, when the English artist Thomas Daniell drew (and later published) a plan of it – a readily available document that was strangely overlooked in earlier discussions about what was or might have been on the site. A later map of the city, published by Muhammad Latif, does not show the garden but the relevant area is labelled 'Mihtab Bagh', suggesting that a memory of the name survived locally (a fact that did not deflect Latif himself from adhering to the second-Taj theory).

The work of the excavators ought logically to put an end to all further talk of the Black Taj. But one rather doubts that things will prove so straightforward. Myths of this kind have an astonishing vitality. Even Thomas Daniell, who measured and drew the Mahtab Bagh whilst camping in it, repeats the story of the second Taj, without making any attempt to reconcile the two ideas, or even showing an awareness that they contradict one another. And the fact that the garden has been shown to have contained an octagonal pool of roughly the same dimensions as the ground plan of the Taj will no doubt encourage some to fancy that it marks the foundation of a second building, after all. The excavators offer the more likely explanation that it was intended to catch the Taj's reflection.

In one sense, the true story of the Mahtab Bagh is even more astonishing than the myth. It is clear from the (now comprehensible) references to it in the Mughal sources that it was built at the same time as the Taj itself. It has been described as a place from which to view the Taj. The tomb's appearance from across the river is certainly stunning (and well worth the detour required to reach the spot). But the Mahtab Bagh is more than a viewing place – more even than a midnight retreat, as its romantic name suggests – it is an integral part of the larger design. The Taj Mahal is always described as standing at the *end* of its garden as opposed to in the middle. But if we take the Mahtab Bagh into account, the tomb is seen to be standing between two *char baghs*. Flowing between them is the River Yamuna, which is here co-opted into the garden scheme. A larger or more ambitious embodiment of the Qur'anic vision of the rivers of paradise would be hard to imagine.

STONE FLOWERS

If the designers of the Taj meant us to view it from a distance by moonlight, they certainly also expected us to examine it closely by the light of day. The exquisite details of its surface demand our attention.

The material that encases all parts of the tomb is white marble, from the mines at Makrana in Rajasthan. Some surviving *farmans*, or imperial letters, dated in the 1630s and addressed to Raja Jai Singh of Amber (the same man from whom the land for the Taj was forcibly purchased), require him to assist with the transportation of marble from Makrana to Agra and instruct him to send more marble and more sculptors to work it. One *farman* in the series accuses Jai Singh of detaining sculptors for his own work in Amber, against clear orders to send all available specialists to Agra. Jai Singh was indeed at this time embellishing his palace with a new courtyard in a somewhat Shah Jahani style. The *farmans* are evidence that some of the sculptors who worked on the Taj, as well as the material, were from Rajasthan.

The idea of covering an entire building with white marble was not entirely new. The Jains of Rajasthan had used Makrana marble to create white temples at Mount Abu as much as five hundred years before, and again at Ranakpur in the fifteenth century. Also of this date is the tomb of Hoshang Shah, Sultan of Mandu, the first tomb to be entirely sheathed in marble and all the more remarkable for being the only building at Mandu to make extensive use of the material. A similar effect was achieved a century later at Fatehpur Sikri, where the tomb of Sheikh Salim, the Sufi saint who assured Akbar that he would father sons and in whose honour the city was consequently built, stands out as a single white marble structure in a sea of red sandstone. The tomb of Itimad-ud-Daulah has a white marble exterior, though heavily ornamented with patterns and panels of inlaid stones of various colours.

According to his court historian Abdul Hamid Lahauri, Shah Jahan consciously reserved white marble for buildings associated with himself. In the fort at Agra, he demolished some of the older sandstone palaces that had been built for Akbar and replaced them with his own marble ones, to project his pure heart and spiritual nature. Against this record it is hardly surprising that the same material was chosen for the Taj. But the scale was unprecedented and so, as a result, is its impact. The earlier buildings mentioned are exquisite, but they are also comparatively small, and more manageable. The sheer quantity of white stone that confronts us on entering the garden of the Taj is overwhelming.

As we approach the building and mount the steps under the great arch of the south face, our eye is caught by the dado panels. Here the marble is carved in relief with depictions of flowers, in sprays or clumps, growing out of small mounds of earth. Around the edges of each panel runs a multi-coloured border with stylised flowers made up of inlaid stones. This scheme is continued on the dados inside the building's central hall, though here some of the carved flowers are depicted as cut stems arranged in vases, and the inlaid borders are more elaborate. The coloured stones include jasper, jade, turquoise, lapis lazuli, coral, cornelian, onyx and amethyst. The juxtaposition of two different techniques – the monochromatic bas-relief carving and the coloured inlay decoration – is surprisingly successful, because of the common floral theme.

In the centre of the hall stands Mumtaz's cenotaph, with that of Shah Jahan alongside it to the west. These are, in fact, empty boxes: the real sarcophagi containing their bodies lie in a crypt directly below, so that they are buried at ground level, though in the same arrangement as the cenotaphs above. It is an arrangement that puts Shah Jahan closer to Mecca and Mumtaz on her husband's left, the side of his heart.

The cenotaphs are enclosed by an octagonal perforated screen. The original screen was made of gold. Fearful that it would sooner or later be looted, Shah Jahan prudently replaced it with the present marble one in 1643 when the tomb was completed. The posts and beams of the screen and the surfaces of the cenotaphs carry the richest of the inlaid decoration, work of such fine craftsmanship and subtle design that it has excited almost as much admiration over the centuries as the building itself.

It has also generated a fair amount of controversy and hot air. The technique of creating patterns or pictures by inlaying coloured stones in a stone surface is of European origin, and is widely known as pietra dura. It is quite distinct from mosaic, which involves sticking pieces of coloured stone adjacently on a common background, and which has various ancient sources. The inlay process of pietra dura is more like marquetry in woodwork, and indeed in Italy the technique was mostly applied to items of furniture. By some means that are admittedly not entirely clear, Mughal craftsmen learnt this technique. It is known that Shah Jahan possessed some specimens of Italian work of this kind: some panels from a cabinet were incorporated into a large design behind the throne in the Hall of Public Audience in Delhi in the 1640s. Since European diplomats and traders at the Mughal court frequently presented works of art and novelties in their attempts to attract the emperor's attention, we may guess that these pieces belonging to Shah Jahan were not the only examples of Italian pietra dura to reach the Mughal court, and that its craftsmen therefore had specimens to study and to imitate.

This explanation contrasts with an earlier popular belief that Italian craftsmen must have travelled to India to teach the Mughals how to do pietra dura, or perhaps that they even executed it themselves on buildings including the Taj. This theory was once vigorously promoted in an effort to establish a measure of European influence, even direct workmanship, in the creation of the Mughal masterpiece. It marks one episode in the history of European responses to the Taj which will be considered in the next chapter, and it was to lead some to declare that the Taj must have been designed and built by Italians.

A complicating factor is that some of the designs (as well as the technique) of Mughal work do seem to have European

14. Flowers carved in relief and inlaid in pietra dura on a dado on the exterior of the Taj Mahal.

sources. Elements of the borders around the dados are strongly reminiscent of Mannerist 'strapwork' designs, and some of the flowers, including those carved in relief, are clearly derived from the depiction of plants in European 'herbals' or botanical studies. These connections too have been seized on by those keen to detect a European contribution. But what such parallels indicate is the involvement not so much of European craftsmen but of European *books*. Images printed in Europe circulated widely in Mughal India and artists studied them for inspiration; it is natural to suppose that they assimilated strapwork and herbals in the same manner. But we might notice that the adoption by Mughal artists of foreign motifs characteristically involved some modification or translation, and in both these cases it entailed a change of medium: strapwork – a monochrome relief pattern in northern Europe – became inlaid and coloured in India whilst the flat drawn flowers of herbals were raised in carved relief.

They took liberties with nature, too. Whilst some of the flowers are recognisable – notably the irises – others seem to be invented, and others again are plainly so, as they combine blooms of different forms and colours on the same stem. Distinguishing the real from the fanciful is not always easy, as they are all depicted in the same free-flowing naturalistic manner, a naturalism that perhaps reflects Indian as much as European traditions and sensibilities.

Given their preponderance in the building's ornament, one might ask: why flowers? Some of them, including the irises, carried funerary associations for the Mughals. But more generally, the flowers allowed for a continuity of conception with the surrounding garden. The ephemeral real flowers of the *char bagh* are crystallised into the permanent stone ones in the tomb. Flowers are also a feature of the natural world whose representation is permitted even within orthodox traditions.

The well-known Islamic prohibition against the depiction of people and animals is based on a *hadith*, a tradition in which the Prophet disapproves of the practice. The idea has often been connected with the Qur'anic prohibitions against the representation of God, and hence the condemnation of statues and idols. The common thought is that God is the sole creator, and that any attempt to imitate life in art is to arrogate his distinctive creative role. But whilst the ban on depicting God is non-negotiable, many Muslim patrons in history have selectively ignored the ban on the representation of higher forms of life. Mughal painting includes portraits of men and depictions of animals of the highest levels of naturalism. The orthodox ban was a matter of debate at Akbar's court, with the emperor arguing that an artist's inevitable failure to match the creativity of God could only bring him closer to an understanding of divine power. Even so, distinctions were drawn. Figurative images could be made to illustrate a book of poetry or history, but not a copy of the Qur'an. Depictions of animals might be employed to decorate a dwelling, but not a mosque. Flowers, on the other hand, were permissible almost anywhere. The *hadith* at the root of the matter concludes with the Prophet saying, 'If you have to paint at all, then paint trees and objects that have not a spirit in them.' Mughal theologians agreed that flowers had a general sanction, and were not at variance with a building's religious character.

In the case of the Taj, the religious character was expressed more forcefully by the other component of the ornament, namely the inscriptions of sacred text. The most prominent are the four that surround the great arch in the centre of each side of the building. Together these include the entire text of the thirty-sixth sura of the Qur'an (in a cursive or *sulus* script of Arabic). This sura is sometimes described as the heart of the Qur'an and is particularly recited to the dying. It speaks of God's gifts to mankind as evidence of his power: 'We quicken the earth and bring forth the grain from it, and they eat thereof; and we make in it gardens of the date and the vine; and we cause springs to gush forth in it; that they may eat of its fruits and of the labour of their hands. Will they not therefore be thankful?' It concludes with a promise of eternal life in heaven to the faithful: 'He shall give life to them who gave them being at first, for in all creation is he skilled … So glory be to him in whose hand is sway over all things! And to him shall ye be brought back.' Even more clearly relevant to the purpose of the building and the nature of its setting is another sura from the Qur'an, inscribed on the outer face of the garden's southern gate, at the entrance into the complex. Known as 'The Daybreak', this sura concludes with the lines:

> Oh, thou soul which art at rest,
> Return to thy Lord, pleased, and pleasing him;
> Enter thou among my servants
> And enter thou my Paradise.

THE PROCESS

Jean-Baptiste 'Two-Taj' Tavernier says that he 'witnessed the commencement and the accomplishment of this great work' and that it took in total twenty-two years. Again he has been widely cited but he is not altogether a reliable witness: he first reached India only in 1640, nearly a decade after construction of the Taj had begun. The last dated inscription in the complex gives a date corresponding to 1647/8, suggesting a time span closer to seventeen years.

Mughal sources give the total cost as fifty *lakhs*, that is five million rupees. It is hard to get an accurate sense of the value of such a sum at the time. According to some economic historians the annual revenue received by the imperial treasury in the early seventeenth century was approximately a hundred million rupees. Of this, 80 per cent was spent on the salaries of the *mansabdars*, the officials and bureaucrats of the empire. Less than 5 per cent was spent on the imperial household, including its building projects. This means that the cost of the Taj is roughly comparable to one full year's expenditure on the household budget (though actually of course spread out over many). In short, it was an expensive building, but it hardly compares with the massive costs of constructing fortifications, especially during Akbar's reign, which saw the building of enormous forts at Agra, Allahabad, Lahore, Attock and elsewhere. Nor does it compare with the cost of warfare, always the largest component of a state's budget. The Mughals were prodigal builders, but they could afford to be. Even a project on the scale of the Taj, involving the distant transportation of masses of stone, presented no kind of threat to the Mughal economy.

A subject on which the Mughal sources are surprisingly less forthcoming than they are about its cost is the identity of its architects. To whom does the credit go for the design of this spectacular work? There is a measure of uncertainty,

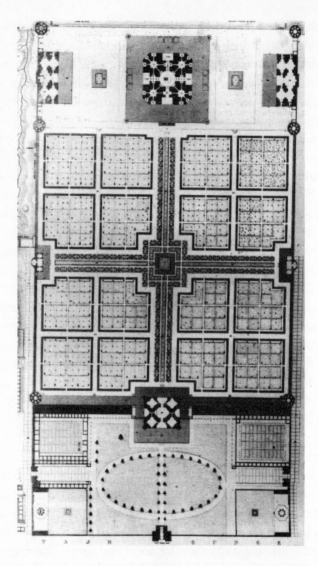

15. Plan of the tomb and garden complex, drawn by Pyari Lal and J. Biswas for the Surveyor General, and published by the Royal Asiatic Society in 1843.

which partly reflects the lower level of esteem accorded to the architectural profession in the Mughal world than in our own. By contrast, many of the painters who worked in the Mughal ateliers we know by name, either because the emperor held them in sufficiently high regard to mention them in his memoirs, or more prosaically because the artists got to sign their work. It is easier to sign a painting than a building. Significantly, the inscriptions on the Taj are signed, because of the very high value given to the art of calligraphy. So in this matter there is no doubt: the calligrapher of the Qur'anic inscriptions on the Taj was one 'Abd-ul-Haq, known as Amanat Khan.

Shah Jahan's official historian, Abdul Hamid Lahauri, names two other men, Mir 'Abd-ul-Karim and Makramat Khan, as the administrators responsible for overseeing the construction of the Taj. The question here is what function Lahauri means to describe. Does an administrator actually design, or merely supervise designers, as might a minister of planning? The credit for the design itself was claimed for one Ustad Ahmad Lahauri, by his son Lutfullah, and this is now generally accepted in spite of the partisan source, because Ustad Ahmad is independently known to have worked on other projects for Shah Jahan, including the Red Fort in Delhi.

There is a consensus on these four names – one architect, one calligrapher, two administrators – but we know disappointingly little about their working methods. There are no records of meetings between Shah Jahan and them, or between them and their workforce. No original drawings or plans survive, though it is inconceivable that a building such as the Taj could have been designed and built without them.

We know only enough to debunk some of the myths. Given that Ustad Ahmad went on to work in Delhi it is evidently not true, as some of the guides still tell us, that Shah Jahan ordered the architect's hands to be cut off to prevent him from working for anyone else.

The agreement that Ustad Ahmad was the architect is of recent date. The late-nineteenth-century author Muhammad Latif claimed to have seen a manuscript which credited one 'Ustad Isa', said to be from Turkey or Persia. This figure turns out to be fictitious, but the name was taken up enthusiastically by other historians such as E. B. Havell, whose main concern was to rebut the idea that it could have been designed by an Italian. And here lies a clue. It has taken so long to achieve clarity on this important matter because assigning authorship for this undoubted masterpiece has always been bound up with the history of European responses to it. That history, to which we now turn, is almost as complex as the story of its creation, and every bit as much a part of the building's life and meaning.

3

EVERYBODY'S TAJ

For a building that is supposedly a symbol of love, the Taj has generated a lot of anger. Or rather, some people have been angered by what others have said about it, and have felt called on to defend its honour. With the consolidation of British imperial power in the nineteenth century, the Taj, as the acknowledged acme of Indian architecture, became caught up in wider disputes about the interpretation of the region's past. From those who claim that India owes its greatness to foreign intervention, to those who insist that all its glories are self-fashioned, every competing idea of India has to accommodate the Taj. Proponents of one cause or another have not felt it sufficient merely to bring the Taj more or less prominently into play, depending on whether it seems to support their argument. Its prominence being guaranteed, they have gone further and tried to co-opt it into telling their particular tale. They have reconstructed it according to their own designs. As a result, the Taj has developed multiple characters and even nationalities.

Perhaps this was always so: the early accounts share a celebratory mood, but there are already some strikingly divergent perspectives.

The earliest appreciations of the Taj Mahal were written in Persian (a courtly and literary language for the Mughals) by Shah Jahan's court historians and poets. The twelfth annual death commemoration (or Urs) of Mumtaz in 1643 also marked the completion of the main buildings. This was the occasion for a detailed description by Abdul Hamid Lahauri in the *Padshahnama*, the official chronicle of the emperor's reign. Lahauri's prose is an uneasy blend of florid metaphor and statistics for the record. About the outer dome, for example, he writes:

Above the inner dome, which is radiant like the hearts of angels, has been raised another heaven-touching, guava-shaped dome, to discover the minute mathematical degrees of which would confound even the celestial geometrician. Crowning this dome of heavenly rank, the circumference of whose outer girth is 110 yards, there has been affixed a golden finial 11 yards high, glittering like the sun, with its summit rising to a total height of 107 yards above the ground.

And later, in a similar vein:

At the corners of the white marble platform, which is 23 yards high above the level of the ground, stand four minarets, also of marble, with interior staircases and capped by cupolas, which are 7 cubits in diameter and rise to a total of 52 cubits from the pavement of the said platform to the finial, appearing, as it were, like ladders reaching towards the heavens.

The chief court poet, Abu Talib Hamadani, writing under

the pen-name Kalim, felt less obliged to impart information. In a series of twenty-four couplets he amasses extravagant metaphors that are free of all taint of measurement. His comparisons range from the third-century religious teacher Mani (traditionally seen by Muslim writers as a painter) to Chinese artists, who were known and revered in India chiefly for their ceramics:

> Upon her grave – may it be illumined till the Resurrection! –
> The King of Kings constructed such an edifice
> That since the Divine Decree drew creation's plan
> No one has seen its equal in magnificence …

> Since heaven's vault has been standing, an edifice like this
> Has never risen to compete against the sky.
> Its colour resembles dawn's bright face
> For both inside and out it is entirely marble.
> Nay, not marble, for in respect of delicacy and beauty
> The eye can mistake it for a cloud.

> On its stones, a hundred kinds of ornaments and designs
> Have become apparent through the chisel's blade.
> Indeed the chisel has become the fabled brush of Mani,
> Painting a myriad pictures upon the water of the marble …
> The embellishment of its stones has put out the candle
> Of the art and skill of the artists of China.

Kalim was the first author to employ the 'words are inadequate' defence, a theme much adopted by later writers fearful that their description might not measure up to the building. His version is a falsely modest reworking of an established Persian trope:

In its praise, Speech need not resort to elaboration –
The very device that is the poet's stock-in-trade.
Elaboration has been exhausted on it on so vast a scale
That for Speech there now remains no share.

Others concentrated less on the tomb's appearance than
on its religious resonance. Kalim's rival at court, the poet
Muhammad Jan, known as Qudsi, plays on the paradise
imagery:

Houris, adorned with scented beauty marks
Continually sweep its courtyard with the brooms of their eyelashes.

On this holy edifice of lofty station
The cloud of divine mercy continually showers moisture.

There are different emphases here, but each of these court
authors invokes ideas embedded in Islamic thought. Even
the comparatively dry Lahauri, despite all his numbers, also
deploys angel hearts and heaven-reaching ladders to position
the building securely within Islam. European observers were
less attuned to this field of literary and religious association,
and saw and described the Taj quite differently – not as one
expression of Islamic ideas to be related to other such expressions, but as a building to be compared with other buildings.

The most interesting, as well as the fullest, early European
account is by François Bernier, the itinerant French physician,
in a letter written from Delhi in 1663. Addressing a compatriot who has not visited India, Bernier is at pains to compare
each part of the complex to landmark buildings in Paris. The
outer courtyard is said to be larger than the Place Royale, and

the façade of the entrance gate is wider and grander than that of Saint Louis in the rue Saint Antoine, whilst the dome of the Taj itself is reckoned to be 'nearly of the same height as the Val-de-Grâce'. Against these favourable comparisons, it worries Bernier a little that the buildings do not adhere to the Western classical style and he concedes that 'the columns, the architraves and the cornices are, indeed, not formed according to the proportion of the five orders of architecture so strictly observed in French edifices'. A Mughal building 'is of a different and peculiar kind; but not without something pleasing in its whimsical structure; and in my opinion it well deserves a place in our books of architecture'.

Bernier feels himself to be appreciative against his own better judgement. Unencumbered by any notion of pluralism, he supposes Europe's classical orders to be universal norms from which a deviation is a lapse. Liking Mughal architecture regardless, he suspects the lapse to be in his own discernment and twice admits that 'I may have imbibed an Indian taste'. Luckily, he has a chance to test this deterioration against a compatriot less affected than himself. As he explains:

> The last time I visited Tage Mehale's mausoleum I was in the company of a French merchant [generally assumed to have been the diamond trader Jean-Baptiste Tavernier], who, as well as myself, thought that this extraordinary fabric could not be sufficiently admired. I did not venture to express my opinion, fearing that my taste might have become corrupted by my long residence in the Indies; and as my companion was come recently from France, it was quite a relief to my mind to hear him say that he had seen nothing in Europe so bold and majestic.

Inside the tomb, Bernier admires the pietra dura work, which reminds him of 'the Grand Duke's chapel at Florence', and he notes that mullahs are employed to read aloud from the Qur'an continuously, 'in respectful memory of Tage Mehale' – and of her alone, because at the time of his visit Shah Jahan was still alive, under house arrest in the fort. Her tomb – her real sarcophagus in the vault below the hall with the cenotaph – he is not permitted to see: it was opened only once a year and even then Christians were not admitted.

That Bernier's unnamed companion was indeed Tavernier is more or less confirmed by the latter's own description of the tomb, included in his volume of travel memoirs published in 1676, where he compares the dome to that of the Val-de-Grâce: it was obviously a point that the two Parisians had discussed. However ethnocentric such comparisons might seem, the international note is not inappropriate, for it was Tavernier's conviction that Shah Jahan fully intended the Taj to have a wide audience, 'that the whole world should see and admire its magnificence'.

COMPANY & CROWN

The French were the first Europeans to respond to the Taj but as the East India Company expanded its sphere of influence across northern India in later centuries the predominant voices were British. The diplomat Sir Charles Malet – the man who dubbed it 'the wonder of the Eastern world' – was one of a trickle of travellers in the late eighteenth century, others being deterred by the instability of the region around Agra, then under the control of the Marathas, against whom the Company waged a series of wars. For Malet, at least according to his friend James Forbes, 'This building, in point of design and execution, is one of the most extensive, elegant, commodious and perfect works that was ever undertaken and finished by one man.'

With the expulsion of the Marathas and the capture of Agra by forces under Lord Lake in 1803, the city became more accessible and foreign visitor numbers increased. Their attitude, though consistently admiring, was not wholly reverential. In the early nineteenth century the Taj was seen by the British as a pleasure resort. Banquets were held in the Mihman Khana or Jawab – the building facing the tomb from the east – and dance parties were held on the terrace. Some visitors carved their names on the walls of the monument, more elegantly than modern vandals perhaps, but hardly with greater respect. As the viceroy Lord Curzon later complained, 'It was not an uncommon thing for the revellers to arm themselves with hammer and chisel with which they whiled away the afternoon by chipping out fragments from the cenotaphs of the Emperor and his late lamented Queen.' Perhaps they thought they were acting with historical precedent: it was widely believed that troops from a Jat garrison that occupied Agra in 1764 had picked out some of the semi-precious stones from the pietra dura panels and had looted the tomb's original silver doors.

The British idea that, being in charge, they were free to do with the Mughal heritage as they pleased persisted for some decades. The Company official Sir William Sleeman – famous for his role in the suppression of *thuggee* or highway robbery – records the fate of the veranda of the *hammam* in the Agra fort:

16. The 'Composition Piece' painted by Thomas Daniell for Thomas Hope in 1799; a capriccio showing the Taj with other Indian buildings, which typifies the Georgian combination of inquiry and fantasy.

The Marquis of Hastings, when Governor-General of India [1813–23], broke up one of the marble baths of this palace to send home to George IV of England, then Prince Regent; and the rest of the suite of apartments from which it had been taken, with all its exquisite fretwork and mosaic, was afterwards sold by auction, on account of our government, by order of the then Governor-General, Lord W[illiam] Bentinck [1828–35]. Had these things fetched the price expected, it is probable that the whole of the palace, and even the Taj itself, would have been pulled down, and sold in the same manner.

The break-up and sale of parts of the *hammam* has been investigated by Ebba Koch, who was able to locate many of the parts (some of which have never left Agra). It seems Sleeman was quite correct about these events. His further comment about pulling down the Taj is the basis of a now widespread belief that the British seriously planned to dismantle it. But this is to misread the tone: his remark is a sarcastic exaggeration, a cynical rebuke of those who let their admiration lead to plunder.

Sleeman is similarly contemptuous of the 'quadrille and tiffin parties' held by his compatriots at the Taj. His own response was more high minded. He summed up the building as 'a faultless congregation of architectural beauties on which [the mind] could dwell for ever without fatigue … I went on from part to part in the expectation that I must by and by come to something that would disappoint me; but no, the emotion which one feels at first is never impaired.'

He then courteously turned to his wife to ask her what she thought. '"I cannot," said she, "tell you what I think, for I know not how to criticise such a building, but I can tell you what I feel. I would die tomorrow to have such another over me!"'

This remark has sometimes been quoted as an example of the European Romantic sensibility at work in India. Fair enough in a sense, but that is to overlook Lady Sleeman's nice distinction between 'think' and 'feel'. Her claim that she does not know 'how to criticise' the Taj is not quite the same as her husband's inability to find fault (try as he might). Rather she is candidly confessing her ignorance of the appropriate aesthetic canon, of the architectural rules at play. She is in fact rather astutely recognising cultural difference, that the Taj is Islamic and not neoclassical. The implication is that if called on to do so she would know perfectly well how to criticise a seventeenth-century building in England – St Paul's Cathedral perhaps – but that such a skill does not apply.

Lady Sleeman's awareness of the need for pluralism when making aesthetic judgements sets her apart from others of her time. More typical is Maria, wife of Sir George Nugent, the commander-in-chief of the Bengal army. She visited the monument in November 1812 and recalled:

In spite of my high expectations, it greatly exceeded them – it is quite impossible to describe it ... We took three hours to examine it in the minutest detail. I could look at it for as many months, without being tired – it is really like the most beautiful Sèvres china, and deserves to have a glass case made for it.

Lady Nugent was one of many who felt compelled to visit by all that she had been told about the Taj, and was still surprised rather than disappointed by the experience. This becomes a common refrain. Reginald Heber, Bishop of Calcutta, visited in 1825 and reported:

> *I went to see the celebrated Tage-mahal, of which it is enough to say that, after hearing its praises ever since I had been in India, its beauty rather exceeded than fell short of my expectations. There was much, indeed, which I was not prepared for.*

A contender with Lady Sleeman in the tendency to identify with Mumtaz, and thus to consider one's own future death, is the spirited adventurer and traveller Fanny Parks, who visited in 1835 and concludes her description with a personalised address:

> *And now adieu, beautiful Taj, adieu! In the far, far West I shall rejoice that I have gazed upon your beauty, nor will the memory depart until the lowly tomb of an English gentlewoman closes on my remains.*

The later nineteenth century produced some more sober and scholarly, less passionate responses from the British. A *History of Indian and Eastern Architecture*, published in 1876 by the Victorian polymath James Fergusson, is widely regarded as the first modern study of the history of Indian architecture, in the sense that it was the first work to attempt a comprehensive narrative, assigning buildings to chronological periods and working out the relations between them in terms of stylistic influence and technological development. His description of the Taj in this book is certainly more analytical than those offered by his Georgian predecessors, though hardly less enthusiastic:

No building in India has been so often drawn and photographed as this, or more frequently described; but, with all this, it is almost impossible to convey an idea of it to those who have not seen it, not only because of its extreme delicacy, and the beauty of the material employed in its construction, but from the complexity of the design. If the Taj were only the tomb itself, it might be described, but the platform on which it stands, with its tall minarets, is a work of art in itself. Beyond this are the two wings, one of which is a mosque, which anywhere else would be considered an important building. This group of buildings forms one side of a garden court 880ft square; and beyond this again an outer court ... contains in the centre of its inner wall the great gateway of the garden court, a worthy pendant to the Taj itself. Beautiful as it is in itself, the Taj would lose half its charm if it stood alone. It is the combination of so many beauties, and the perfect manner in which each is subordinated to the other, that makes up a whole which the world cannot match, and which never fails to impress even those who are most indifferent to the effects produced by architectural objects in general.

Fergusson has been much reviled by those who came later. The early-twentieth-century arts teacher and author E. B. Havell, who was more inclined to artistic enthusiasm than to academic precision, was impatient with Fergusson's systematic definitions. 'The history of architecture is not, as Fergusson thought, the classification of buildings in archaeological water-tight compartments according to arbitrary academic ideas of style,' he grumbled sarcastically, 'but a history of national life and thought.' He did not explain quite how architecture expresses 'national life': he preferred inclusive vagueness to judgemental distinctions. His particular grouse here was with Fergusson's classification of the Taj as 'Indian Saracenic', a label that in Havell's view overstressed its foreign component.

Fergusson's pioneering role in the discipline has also made him a target for postcolonial critics, who argue that his supposed admiration for Indian design was suffused by attitudes of colonial mastery. It has to be conceded that he made his critics' task easy. At the Taj he praised the pietra dura decoration, only to conclude: 'Though, of course, not to be compared with the intellectual beauty of Greek ornament, it certainly stands first among the purely decorative forms of architectural design.' And of the Taj in general he summarised: 'Its beauty may not be of the highest class, but in its class it is unsurpassed.'

There is something grudging about this, though it is also true that such comments are parts of an attempt to sustain a wider argument that runs through his book. In a much discussed passage Fergusson compares the Parthenon and the Hindu temple of Halebid, only to conclude that they are not comparable; that they represent polar ends of a spectrum, as their architects were trying to achieve quite different things. Fergusson is arguing for pluralism here, suggesting the need to identify different criteria for assessment. But his proposition that the Parthenon embodies 'pure refined intellectual power' where the Hindu temple embodies 'all that is wild in human faith or warm in human feeling' implies a preference for the former. Not a spectrum, then, but a scale. The detail undoes his general purpose to 'widen our basis for architectural criticism'.

Nobody today reads Fergusson's book for information or for pleasure. He has become a whipping boy, read only by those seeking proof of his guilt. It is worth acknowledging, then, that he was the first art historian correctly to identify the Taj as belonging to a tradition rather than as something unique, and the first author to analyse at any length a point that had struck others previously: that the effect of the Taj depends as much on the architectural ensemble as on the design of the tomb alone.

THE VERONEO AFFAIR

The decades before and after 1900 saw a revival of one of the most far-fetched ideas ever made about the Taj, namely that Europeans were involved in its design. The basis of this controversy is a comment made by a Portuguese Augustinian friar named Father Sebastien Manrique, who visited Agra in 1640 whilst the construction of the Taj was in progress. He later wrote: 'The architect of these works was a Venetian, by name Geronimo Veroneo, who had come to this part in a Portuguese ship and died in the city of Lahore just before I reached it.'

There is no reasonable ground for anyone to have believed this assertion, at any time. Manrique does not say he knew Veroneo: on the contrary he explicitly states that he reached Lahore too late to meet him, and he is therefore reporting hearsay. Viewed in the context of the other contemporary evidence, it doesn't seem at all plausible. The Englishman Peter Mundy, who did know Veroneo well, mentions the Taj but not his friend as the alleged architect, and the omission (even if this is arguing from absent evidence) tells against the claim. The other European eyewitnesses of the construction – Bernier, Tavernier and Manucci amongst them – similarly give no hint of any European involvement, something that would surely have interested them and their readers if there were any wind of it. Another, Jean de Thévenot, was told that Shah Jahan had appointed a special council of 'all the able architects of the Indies'. Tavernier states that Shah Jahan had sought to employ one Austin or Augustin of Bordeaux for some decorative work on the Agra fort, but he does not link this figure to the Taj.

The idea of European involvement in the design begins to appear in English writing soon after the British capture of Agra in 1803. It was first mentioned by an anonymous Englishwoman (known only as 'A.D.'), who visited in 1808 and published an account in 1823, and by the artist Charles Ramus Forrest, who was also in Agra in 1808 and published in 1824. William Sleeman, publishing in 1844, attributes not only the Taj but the palaces of both Agra and Delhi to Austin of Bordeaux, who he says also went by the name 'Oosten Esau'. Fanny Parks was obviously amongst his readers as she repeats every particular in her travel book first published in 1850.

There for a while the matter rested. But Manrique's claim for Veroneo was picked up and popularised in a *Guide to Agra* published in 1888 by H. G. Keene. This may have been unwitting on Keene's part. In an earlier edition of his guide he had rejected any possibility of European contribution; but in the new edition he states it as a fact whilst simultaneously pointing out that the style of the building alone belies the claim. The idea evidently appealed to some of Keene's readers more than it did to him; and he muddied the waters by suggesting, in his *Guide to Delhi* of 1882, that the pietra dura work in the Delhi fort was by Austin of Bordeaux. Further excitement was caused by the rediscovery in 1910 of Veroneo's grave in Agra, putting him at the scene.

17. Detail of Itimad-ud-Daulah's tomb; typical of the work that some Britons could not believe was executed by Indians, and which Lutyens regarded as a 'vertical tile floor'.

The controversy that followed was not entirely academic. It arose in part from an evident desire on the part of some Britons to claim a stake in an undoubted masterpiece, and from a reluctance to admit that Indians could have been capable of producing anything so fine without European assistance. It also reflected the extent to which, if not the building itself, at least its recent fame was felt to be a product of the West. Of course, Indian writers were celebrating the Taj too in this period. The Bengali Nobel laureate Rabindranath Tagore composed a poem in which he memorably described the tomb as 'a teardrop on the cheek of time', and Muhammad Latif published a book on Agra in 1896. More generally, Indians visited the Taj in large numbers in the nineteenth century – an internal tourist trade that cut across the regional and class divisions of Indian society. But the British had their own tradition of visiting and admiring the Taj, which did not depend on Indian participation. The Taj had become part of a British experience of India. A people who could sing patriotically about Jerusalem would not find it hard to see the Taj as their own.

The most vociferous proponent of European involvement in its design was Vincent Smith. In his *History of Fine Art in India and Ceylon*, first published in 1911, he covers the controversy in some detail. He begins with seeming impartiality by stating that some contemporary Persian manuscripts name the chief architect as Ustad Isa, also known as Muhammad Isa Effendi (information that he had obviously lifted from Muhammad Latif's book). But he then asserts that Muslim authors are notoriously biased towards members of their own faith, and advances as more dependable the rival theory from Manrique, naming Veroneo. The standard objection – that the building is not remotely European in style – does not impress him, as Smith points out that a clever Venetian could have adopted an 'Asiatic' style (whatever that may mean). So, he sticks by his long-held view that 'the incomparable Taj is the product of a combination of European and Asiatic genius'.

This conclusion is plainly not warranted by the scanty evidence, but equally obviously Smith's main if undeclared aim was to claim a stake for Europe and to belittle Indian workmanship. He lets this slip when triumphantly pointing out: 'It should be observed that no authority ascribes the design to an Indian architect': he was either Veroneo, who was a European, or Ustad Isa who was 'probably a Turk' (actually he was fictitious). The attitude is consistent with much of the rest of his book, causing a later editor to remark candidly about its author, 'the criticism of art was never his chief care'. In another work Smith famously declared that Indian sculpture 'hardly deserves to be reckoned as art'.

He wasn't quite finished. In 1915 Smith published a new edition of Sleeman's memoirs. In an editorial note he ticks off Sleeman for suggesting Austin of Bordeaux as the architect (an idea that he says Sleeman got from Tavernier). He then goes on to advance again the claim for Veroneo. He quotes himself: 'Personally, I am of opinion, as I was more than twenty years ago, that "the incomparable Taj is the product of a combination of European and Asiatic genius".' And he adds gleefully: 'That opinion makes some people very angry.'

The person most inflamed by it was E. B. Havell, the pugnacious director of the Calcutta School of Art and self-appointed defender of Indian art against Western influence and Western imputations about its quality. In the second edition of his *Guide to Agra* (1912) Havell attacks Smith for needlessly reviving the Veroneo controversy, and hotly denies any Western influence on Indian art (whilst also, somewhat self-contradictorily, denouncing its effects where it occurred).

Havell's subsequent and more substantial *History of Indian Architecture* (1913) is a sustained and spirited rant with a variety of objectives, including the hope of persuading the government of India that the design of New Delhi should be entrusted to Indian architects rather than to Edwin Lutyens. He briefly whipped up considerable support for this suggestion, amongst artists and writers, but his high-placed opponents doubted that any capable Indian architects existed – an assertion that Havell points out would be, if true, a terrible indictment of British architectural and educational policies.

The central argument of the book, however, is to deny the existence of outside influences on Indian architecture in general. Any feature that appeared to have been introduced from outside – such as the Islamic pointed arch – is said to have 'really' been first invented in India, exported, and then re-imported into India, its homeland, where it had been forgotten but was embraced like a returning prodigal. He argues that Islamic architecture in India is entirely derived from Indian precedents, owing little or nothing to Islamic architecture abroad. The archaeologist will 'search in vain in central Asia, Persia, Arabia, Egypt or in Europe for Saracenic buildings which explain either the symbolism or the constructive principles of the great Muhammadan buildings in India. The true history of Indian architecture, Buddhist, Hindu and Muhammadan, is written in the monuments which exist only in India itself.'

The spectacle of an author being carried away by his own rhetoric is painful to the sympathetic reader. His intentions were sound: he sought to correct an earlier prejudice that identified the high points of Indian civilisation with the moments of its contact with Europe, starting with the brief incursion by Alexander the Great in 326 BC. It was even believed by some that the representation of Hindu gods and goddesses in human form was a legacy of Greek art. The notion that Indians needed to be shown by European example how to see and depict their own deities merits a prize for effrontery. Havell's impatience with any such ideas was understandable, but his insistence on the complete autonomy of Indian art merely presented the opposite extreme and persuaded no one.

The debate between Smith and Havell did not end with them, and its element of the absurd provides an instructive context in which to view some later assessments that over-emphasise either the foreign or the indigenous roots of Indian art in general and of the Taj in particular. This argument was still going on, and was hardly less polarised, in the late twentieth century. In an otherwise balanced and readable book on Mughal cities published in 1968, Gavin Hambly, for example, describes the Taj as 'perhaps the greatest single achievement of Safavid art', referring to the Persian dynasty that was contemporary with the Mughals. This definition is ludicrous: much as the design of the Taj complex incorporates ideas that are of Persian origin, there is no Safavid building that is remotely similar, and Mughal culture in general is quite distinct. At the other end of the spectrum, the Indian writer Ram Nath in 1972 claimed that the Taj 'is not a monument of Islam' in the strict sense, having been 'produced in accordance with our ancient *vastu* canons', a reference to Sanskrit texts on Hindu architecture. In his attempt to demonstrate this, he uses inappropriate Sanskrit terms to describe the building's parts. The plan is said to be a *sarvato bhadra*, and the terrace is called a *jagati*, but any reader who compares the forms of the building with these typologies as defined in the texts will be baffled by the supposed connections. There *is* a traditional Indian plan type called *sarvato bhadra*, but the Taj is not an example of it; and a *jagati* is the platform of a temple. The giveaway word in Nath's analysis is 'our': the argument is motivated by the desire to claim the Taj exclusively for India.

More balanced analyses must lie between these two extremes and acknowledge the broad range of sources, both foreign and indigenous, blended in a manner that could only have been achieved on Indian soil under Mughal patronage.

BUT IS IT ARCHITECTURE?

When Edwin Lutyens arrived in Delhi in 1912 to plan the new imperial city and to design Viceroy's House, he was told that the viceroy of the time, Lord Hardinge, 'for high considerations of state, felt bound to have an Indian styled city'. This was not at all what Lutyens wished to hear: one style alone was suitable for such a work, namely Europe's own classical tradition. Was the greatest commission of his career going to be spoilt by the ignorant and pretentious intervention of a statesman? Hardinge was in earnest though and sent Lutyens off on study tours to Agra, Jaipur and Mandu, so that he might learn the principles of Mughal, Rajput and sultanate architecture. On his return from this unlooked-for research opportunity, Lutyens delivered a one-word report: 'Piffle.'

18. Viceroy's House (now Rashtrapati Bhawan) designed by
Edwin Lutyens, 1912–31.

For the amusement of Herbert Baker, his collaborator on the project, he wrote a note on how to do Mughal architecture:

Build a vasty mass of rough concrete, elephant-wise, on a very simple rectangular-cum-octagon plan, dome in anyhow, cutting off square. Overlay with a veneer of stone patterns, like laying a vertical tile floor, and get Italians to help you. Inlay jewels and cornelians if you can afford it and rob someone if you can't. Then on top of the mass put three turnips in concrete and overlay with stone or marble as before. Be very careful not to bond anything in, and don't care a damn if it does all come to pieces.

Behind the arrogant wit and the historical misconception about Italians there lurks a serious point. During his reluctant studies he had encountered buildings which were simply not architecture as he understood it. In the stone traditions of classical Europe, the stone itself is the main constructive material. Stone columns support stone lintels, walls are composed of stone blocks, and arches are formed of interlocking stone voussoirs. If the material is to be brick – as in many Roman fortifications – then it is revealed as such. In either case the skill lies in the handling of the material and in the legibility of the constructive principles. But in many of the Indian buildings that Lutyens saw, he detected no such clarity or rigour, as the stone was laid over the top of a brick wall or arch and the construction was concealed. This is true also of the Taj Mahal, for though it is invariably described as being built of marble, one might more accurately say that it is built of brick and rubble and then faced with marble, both inside and out. The marble is a casing that hangs on the building, and its structure lies within. Theoretically one could remove all the marble and the building would still be there.

To Lutyens – taking a somewhat purist and parochial view of the matter – this means that Mughal buildings including the Taj do not qualify as architecture at all. 'Personally I do not believe there is any real Indian architecture,' he declared. What he had seen was merely 'veneered joinery in stone'. But Ustad Ahmad, the architect of the Taj, was not trying to imitate Roman architecture. His method employs principles derived from west Asian and Indian traditions. A building in Persia, for example, might be constructed in brick and then covered in glazed tiles, a cladding that is both protective and ornamental. Adapting this approach to Indian conditions, the tiles are replaced with stone because of its ready availability and the locally developed skills in quarrying, cutting and dressing it. The Taj is by no means the first example of such a combination: it had been used in Indian buildings of many types since the early fourteenth century.

A different kind of doubt about the status of the Taj as architecture arises from the persistent habit amongst critics to anthropomorphise the building, and specifically to see it as 'feminine'. Though it had been suggested many times before, this idea was developed furthest by Percy Brown, an arts educator who was successively director of the School of Art in Calcutta, curator of the Victoria Memorial Hall in the same city and adviser on paintings for Viceroy's House in New Delhi. He was a sober man: holiday snapshots show him fishing in Kashmir, standing midstream in a three-piece suit. In 1942 he published a two-volume study of Indian architecture, the first comprehensive survey of the subject since

Fergusson's, which is still used as a work of reference. It is rather dry, until he reaches the Taj Mahal.

Seeing it half-veiled from the garden, Brown suggests, makes apparent its 'character of femininity', which he considers to be 'intentional as a tribute to the sex of the royal personage it enshrines'. The effect is caused by several features: the 'soft moulding of its contours, the superfine treatment of its decoration, and the chaste texture and subtle colouring of its material, which, combined with the gracious and poetical nature of the building as a whole, all tend to imply a humanity which can only be feminine'. He is a very gallant lover. It occurs to him, though, that the people who built it were also perhaps a bit effeminate: 'On the other hand the fact should not be overlooked that the Mughals themselves had passed beyond that stage of robustness and masculine virility that distinguished their early period and were now experiencing that season of mellow sensuousness', brought on by political and economic security. 'In such circumstances it is more than probable that not a little of the effeminate quality of this building was merely an expression of the spirit of the time.'

Part woman, part zeitgeist; it is seemingly too prosaic to see the Taj as mere architecture.

BEGLEY'S THRONE

Others have been tempted to see the Taj as something more than architecture, as though 'just a tomb' is inadequate as an explanation of its scale and splendour. The most ambitious and scholarly attempt to attribute a further significance to it was made by the Mughal specialist Wayne E. Begley. In a celebrated article published in 1979, Begley proposed that the tomb is a symbolic replica of the Throne of God, the seat on which God will sit in judgement at the Resurrection. In Islamic cosmology this throne, called 'Arsh, is situated on a plinth and is supported by four pillars; beneath it lies the celestial garden which the faithful will enter to witness the vision of God. Representing these parts, the Taj complex is therefore 'a vast allegory of the Day of Resurrection'.

The main obstacle in the way of proving that any such symbolism was intended is the scarcity of other representations of the Throne of God with which it might be compared. They are scarce because a depiction of the Throne would be almost as much a heresy as a depiction of God himself. Nevertheless, Begley points to a treatise by the thirteenth-century Sufi mystic Ibn al-'Arabi (the manuscript of which is in Istanbul) which contains some schematic diagrams of the Throne and the 'Plain of Assembly' for the faithful, and he indicates supposed correspondences between their forms and the plan of the tomb and garden of the Taj.

Begley's argument has not persuaded many colleagues in the field, but the rigour and passion with which he makes his case command respect and some have felt inclined to admit his interpretation as a possibility. The idea has also begun to appear in popular guidebooks. In my own view it is not sustainable for a variety of reasons. In the first place the alleged source of the imagery, Ibn al-'Arabi's manuscript, is highly esoteric and there is no evidence that either it or anything comparable was known in Mughal India. More importantly, even if it were known to both the patron and his architect, it was not sufficiently widely known to function successfully as a symbolic reference.

There is a broader point here about the manner in which

architecture carries meaning. Buildings convey meanings to audiences through their physical resemblance to other things – notably earlier buildings – that have been imbued with particular associations; but they can achieve this successfully only if the associations attached to the point of reference are widely shared and understood. So, for example, neoclassical buildings, such as the British Museum or the Lincoln Memorial, convey certain values that are cherished by British and American societies (humanism, justice and learning) because they are seen to resemble the architecture of the classical world which is also traditionally regarded as the ultimate source of those values. When that idea fades (as perhaps it already is doing) this meaning will be lost. The communication depends on a sustained and shared visual vocabulary. Meanings that are cunningly hidden by designers and ingeniously revealed by scholars are not meanings in the public sphere at all. Secret symbols appeal only to cryptologists; they are deliberately intended to elude the rest of us.

The idea of the Throne of God is central to Islamic theology, but a visual depiction of it was not part of the collective Mughal imagination and cannot therefore have been invoked as a point of reference. It simply wouldn't work: people wouldn't get it. The closest point of comparison would have been the thrones of emperors and sultans, which were publicly on view. But even if the Taj resembled these (which it doesn't) it would still only suggest a royal throne, or thrones in general, not the divine one. There is no visual symbol which might have implanted the specific idea of the Throne of God in the public mind, and without it the theory collapses.

Begley's argument also succumbs to the widely felt temptation to treat the Taj as unique, to think that something so exceptional requires an exceptional explanation; whilst in truth the strong visual references that the building makes to many earlier Indo-Islamic tombs would have signalled to a Mughal audience that it belonged to an established tradition that they well understood. It may be very big and very white, but it's plainly just a tomb because it looks like so many other tombs built over the preceding four centuries.

There is a twist though, for Abdul Hamid Lahauri, Shah Jahan's official historian, does indeed compare the Taj to the Throne of God. He doesn't say that the Taj was meant to represent it, but he does say that it is *like* it. Begley is right to resist pouncing on this, recognising that in the conventional hyperbole of Mughal writing the Throne of God was often alluded to as the acme of architecture, and many other buildings, including Akbar's tomb, were similarly compared with it. Saying that a building resembles the Throne of God is like describing the dome as heaven-touching: not to be taken literally. In this sense, perhaps, any building can be like the Throne of God, and again the Taj is not unique.

HOUSE OF CARDS

An altogether more desperate bid to assign a new meaning to the Taj has been made by P. N. Oak in a book with the intriguing title *The Taj Mahal is a Hindu Palace* (1968). In this startling piece of pseudo-scholarship, Oak soberly protests that the Taj is not, as we have all supposed, a seventeenth-century Muslim tomb but a much earlier Hindu structure, 'perhaps built in the 4th century to serve as a palace'.

His starting point is the passage in the *Padshahnama* describing Shah Jahan's purchase of the site for the Taj, land that belonged through inheritance to the maharaja of Amber, Jai Singh I (the same ruler who was later required to assist with the supply of marble and masons). The passage clearly states that there was a house or mansion (*manzil*) on this land, which had been built by an ancestor of Jai Singh's, so the maharaja received compensation in the form of comparable properties. Oak interprets this to mean that the existing house became the tomb: with the addition merely of a few Qur'anic inscriptions over its doorways, the older palace was converted to its new use. So the universally admired Taj is not, after all, one of the greatest glories of Islamic civilisation but further proof of the wonders of ancient Hinduism.

No evidence is offered in support of its redating by thirteen centuries. Jai Singh's ancestor who built the *manzil*, Raja Man Singh, lived in the sixteenth century and was a contemporary and colleague of Akbar's; but this evidently keeps the whole matter too close to the Mughals for Oak's comfort. The fourth century is safely pre-Islamic. Of course this is preposterous: the only stone architecture surviving in India from such an early date is either rock-cut or monolithic, not structural. The technical know-how to create a building with the structural form of the Taj simply did not exist in pre-Mughal India. It would be like assigning a fourth-century date to a photograph, or a combustion engine. Later in his book Oak seems to drop this claim, giving the building instead a twelfth-century date, and an original function as a Shiva temple.

Whatever date and use he opts for (and the argument has shifted about quite a bit with successive editions of the book) he meets the same objection on the basis of the building's style. If it is not a Mughal building, how does it come to bear such strong affinities with other Mughal buildings, such as their earlier tombs and Shah Jahan's palaces in Agra and Delhi? Oak has his answer ready: the fact that it looks like them is proof that they too are all converted Hindu buildings. 'Muslim rulers in India did not raise even a single mansion, canal, fort, palace, tomb or mosque whether of red stone or marble. They only appropriated Hindu buildings and misused them.' If we still have the breath and energy for further argument, we might ask how he accounts for the similarities between those buildings in India generally thought to be Islamic and the buildings of west Asia. Those, he says, are all 'products of Hindu architecture' as well, evidence that Hindu architecture was the first international style.

I was once gently reprimanded by a senior colleague for paying Oak the compliment of bothering to engage with his book at all. It is plainly a work of fantasy and the author's barely concealed motive to denigrate Islamic civilisation is distasteful. The convoluted passages in which he quotes and wilfully misinterprets texts and inscriptions might be useful as an illustration, to alert students to the methods of phoney scholarship. It contains nothing else that is instructive.

But it merits attention because it is far from unique in adopting the mantle of scholarship in an effort to depreciate the Islamic contribution to India. It was by no means the first work to claim a Hindu origin for an Indian building generally recognised as Islamic. Similar claims were advanced as early as the 1840s about the Qutb Minar, the great victory tower that was raised by the Muslim conquerors of Delhi at the close of the twelfth century. Though the tower's design is plainly based on prototypes in Afghanistan, it was attributed instead to the earlier defeated Rajputs. More recently similar pseudo-scholarship has bedevilled the controversy surrounding the demolition of the mosque known as the Babri Masjid in Ayodhya in December 1992. That act of vandalism perpetrated by members of a 'Hindu nationalist' margin remains a sensitive issue in India today. Though it was executed in the name of Hinduism, the majority of Hindus would deplore it. But some of the activists' sympathisers have been inclined to invoke history and archaeology in support of incredible claims that mask political ambitions, and we might be taking an unnecessary risk if we merely let it pass.

It is of course a sort of compliment to the Taj that it spawns polemics like Oak's. So many people seem to want to claim it for their own, because it is so obviously worth having, and they will happily be misled by the slightest clue that seems to bring it closer to them. Much the same goes for the claims made by Vincent Smith and others that its architect was European. The controversialists share with each other – and with the rest of us more passive admirers – a sense that we are confronting an object that will be universally recognised as supremely beautiful. It is therefore perhaps worth concluding, for balance, with one of the few dissenting voices: that of Aldous Huxley. In a travelogue describing a journey through India, published in 1926, Huxley repeatedly expresses an unusual preference for Rajput over Mughal architecture, and complains that buildings such as the Taj were 'the product of a deficiency of fancy, a poverty of imagination'. But this smacks a little too much of an attempt to be original.

4

....

HOW TO MAKE YOUR OWN

Apart from describing it, what do we *do* with the Taj Mahal? 'The emperor with his wealth,' complained the twentieth-century poet Sahir Ludhianvi, 'mocks the passion of poorer men.' No one can create another one.

To artists the Taj presents a special challenge: it arouses their creative instincts whilst warning that any imitation would be feeble. Even so, that has not deterred numerous artists from attempting to respond to the Taj in works of their own. And when it comes to understanding a masterpiece, works which reflect its influence are as important as those which helped inspire it. Marcel Duchamp's take on the *Mona Lisa* (he scrawled a beard and an obscenity on a reproduction) may not be the most sophisticated reaction to a great portrait, but even this gesture now forms a small part of the life and meaning of the work. The closest that the Taj has got to a Duchamp moment is perhaps its appearance in an advertisement for Johnnie Walker Scotch, declaring, 'It has every right to be expensive.' Other responses – in painting, photography and architecture – have been more subtle, and their variety widens the field of the building's meanings.

There is no contemporary Mughal painting of the Taj (though a number of portraits of Shah Jahan survive). One possible exception is a curious and little-noticed image to be found within the complex itself. Above the central inner arch of the mosque that stands on the lower podium, to the west of the Taj, runs a line of white ornamental painted panels. The middle panel includes an outline of a building which resembles the Taj: a large dome rises over a high arch flanked by smaller arches in two tiers and with what may be minarets at the ends. The image floats next to a drawing of a vase, and is repeated on the other side for symmetry – providing a shred of evidence, should anyone want it, in favour of the two-Taj theory (though there is no bridge, and both outlines are in white). If these images do indeed represent the Taj then they are the first depictions of it, most likely being contemporary with the construction of the complex.

Though Mughal artists achieved the highest degree of realism in the representation of people and animals (despite the traditional Islamic prohibition against it), they did not generally apply the same approach to buildings. Architecture for its own sake was apparently not considered a fit subject for painting. The architectural backdrops of a number of court scenes (notably in the illustrated manuscript of the *Padshahnama* that is now in the royal collection at Windsor) appear to show real spaces with the greatest attention to detail, but even these cannot always be satisfactorily related to the actual palace interiors as they survive today. More often the artists have observed some architectural components and used them to devise a schematic rendering to their own design (see illustration 5, p. 34).

Against this general trend are a few paintings on cloth that show Mughal tomb complexes, though their purpose is unclear. Despite their attention to detail, these are not the designers' drawings, which – as remarked – do not survive. In any case they were made at least a hundred years after the buildings, in the mid or late eighteenth century. Whoever was their patron they clearly respond to an interest in the architecture and the layout of the gardens. One of them shows Jahangir's tomb near Lahore (see illustration 12, p.64). Two others depict the Taj complex (one of these is contained in the small museum at the site). In all of them, the garden is depicted in plan, or from above, whilst the major buildings including the tomb are shown in elevation, as if flattened out and lying down on the terrace.

The Taj and its garden are depicted in a similar style but on a smaller scale in a cloth painting that shows the entire city of Agra, made for the Rajput maharaja Sawai Jai Singh II when he was governor of Agra in the early eighteenth century. It has been suggested that Sawai Jai Singh commissioned this map to use as a model when laying out his own new capital at Jaipur. But if this was his intention it was not carried through, as Jaipur is not built on a river and unlike Agra is planned on a grid. It is more likely that the painting was connected with the governor's repair of the city wall, which it also shows. In either case, the Taj is included here not as a subject of artistic interest but as one amongst many points of topographical reference. The idea of making the Taj the main subject of another work of art was a step that required the introduction of a foreign perception.

The first professional British landscape painter to travel in India was William Hodges (1744–97). A former pupil of Richard Wilson's who had served as official artist on board the *Resolution* for Captain Cook's voyage to the South Pacific, he brought to bear on his Indian adventures a broad experience but also a distinctively English conception of architecture as a part of landscape. Between 1780 and 1783 he travelled extensively in northern India, sometimes in the retinue of his patron, Britain's first Governor General in India, Warren Hastings. The drawings that he made along the way were the sources for his later oils and aquatints, whilst his writing includes a volume of travel memoirs published in 1793.

Hodges reached the Taj in February 1783. His thoughts on it, later recounted in his book, are typical of his approach to Indian architecture in general, in combining both factual and sentimental responses. He begins with a detailed description of the tomb's form and situation: 'The plan of this [building] is octagon[al]; the four principal sides opposed to the cardinal points of the compass. In the center of each of the four sides there is raised a vast and pointed arch …' and so on. But with some of the shapes and measurements out of the way, he moves on to describe the scenic context and its impact on his feelings:

> When this building is viewed from the opposite side of the river, it possesses a degree of beauty, from the perfection of the materials and from the excellence of the workmanship, which is only surpassed by its grandeur, extent and general magnificence. The basest material that enters this center part of it is white marble, and the ornaments are of various coloured marbles, in which

there is no glitter: the whole together appears like a most perfect
pearl on an azure ground. The effect is such as, I confess, I never
experienced from any work of art. The fine materials, the beau-
tiful forms, and the symmetry of the whole, with the judicious
choice of situation, far surpasses anything I ever beheld.

The panegyric perhaps disguises the extent to which, more
than most English travellers of his time, Hodges thought
deeply about the architecture that he encountered. Not always
content with wonder, he attempted to analyse it and developed a theory of Indian architecture that he first expressed
in a *Dissertation on the Prototypes of Architecture*, published
in 1787. In view of its dependence on the pointed arch, he
believed Islamic architecture to be related to Gothic, and he
proposed that both are derived from the forms of mountains
and caves, distinguishing them from Western classical architecture which was widely supposed to trace its origin back
to the form of a primitive wooden hut. Style, he argued, is
as much a product of location and climate as of history. This
insight led him in two somewhat contradictory directions: it
enabled him to dethrone Western classicism as the superior or
normative style against which all others had to be measured;
but it also encouraged him to detect supposed connections
across cultures that are at best doubtful. We should not blame
Indian architecture for not being Greek, he argued, whilst
claiming that its common source in mountainous forms links
it with both Gothic and Egyptian architecture.

His sources of information on the Taj were various. Some
were local: he records that 'several mullahs attend the mosque
here at hours of prayer' and that they are 'extremely attentive
to strangers and assiduous to shew and explain every part

of it'. But he also reveals that he had read Tavernier, and he believed the story of the second Taj, adding (perhaps for the first time) the detail of the connecting bridge. There were other myths around at this time too, including the idea that the marble had been brought all the way from Kandahar, in Afghanistan.

Hodges made a number of drawings at the site. His series of aquatints, *Select Views in India* (1785–8), includes a view of the fort in which the silhouette of the distant Taj is visible on the horizon, but he never fulfilled his intention to make the Taj itself the subject of another print in the series. He was perhaps a little intimidated by its perfection. An oil painting that he devoted to the subject (now in the National Gallery of Modern Art in New Delhi) shows the building from across the river – his preferred view. It is large and vigorously painted, but it matches neither the accuracy nor the eloquence of his verbal account. Sadly it shows just how hard it is to capture the outline of the famous dome.

Hodges was followed (as at many other sites) by Thomas and William Daniell, an uncle-and-nephew team who spent seven years in India between 1786 and 1793. Engaged in an artistic rivalry with Hodges, they consciously sought to outdo him in their more thorough, faithful and systematic depiction of Indian architecture for English audiences. According to the daily diary kept by William, they reached the spot on 20 January 1789 and pitched their tents in the Mahtab Bagh. They spent the first day drawing the view from across the river, on the second they crossed over to visit the tomb itself and explored the interior, and on the third day Thomas drew the view from the garden side with the help of a camera obscura whilst William clambered about on the dome.

19. The Taj Mahal from the garden side; aquatint by
Thomas and William Daniell, 1801.

The Daniells too omitted the Taj from their enormous series of aquatints, *Oriental Scenery* (1795–1808), but not from any fear of failure. To treat the subject on the scale they evidently thought it merited, they published in 1801 a supplementary pair of aquatints, each measuring nearly three feet across, depicting the Taj from both the river front and the garden side, together with a plan of the complex and an explanatory booklet. The aquatints are technically amongst the most accomplished pictorial printing of their time.

Like Hodges, the Daniells admired the view of the tomb from across the river because the water 'not only adds to its majesty, but, by reflection, multiplies its splendour'. But they were almost equally struck by its appearance from the garden. Their version of this view 'was taken immediately on entering it by the principal gate', from where the tomb 'has a most impressive effect on the spectator. The large marble basin in the centre of the garden with fountains, and those rising out of the watery channel with paved walks on each side, add to the variety and richness of the scene, and give to it that coolness which is so luxurious an improvement to an Oriental garden.'

They duly give prominence to the pool and its fountains. This has the effect of pushing the tomb itself into the background, where it is overshadowed and partly obscured by foliage. Whenever one work of art serves as the subject for another there is a potential area of aesthetic conflict: the later artist might be inspired by a quite different sense of desired artistic effect from those who created the subject in the first place. That certainly seems to have happened here. The Taj Mahal, being a symmetrical building of uniform colour and smooth finish, set in a formal garden, is about as far removed as it could be from the irregular, varied and rough forms preferred by the English picturesque. An ancient ruin in a natural landscape would have been a more appropriate subject.

The fact is the Taj in itself is not really picturesque in the English sense at all. Recognising this, some commentators have suggested that the Daniells' selection of it as a subject shows that the label does not apply to their work, and that their motive must have been topography, or a quest for the sublime. But this is to grasp the wrong end of the matter. The picturesque admittedly includes a predilection for certain kinds of subject, including ruins, but it is a mode of representation that can be applied to any object, irrespective of its intrinsic qualities. The most reluctant subject can be forced to fit the paradigm. Here, the avenue of cypresses flanking the water channel would certainly be too regular for a picturesque view, so the Daniells have left most of them out, as if they had been torn up, leaving a few stragglers standing about asymmetrically. The tree in the left foreground – of no species known to India – is hardly suggestive of a walled *char bagh* and creates instead the impression that we have stumbled on this scene in a corner of the park of an English country house.

Finding the desired picturesque qualities absent, the Daniells have introduced them. In their writings they repeatedly insist on their concern for accuracy, and they boast of their superiority over Hodges in this regard, but their images no less than his translate Mughal architecture into an aesthetic that was more amenable to a contemporary English audience. This process is inevitable: all artists turn nature into art in the terms that they know. Some postcolonial critics have seen the picturesque as an instrument deliberately wielded to inflict violence on Indian culture by depicting it in a state of ruin. But this view treats artistic creativity as raw ideology, rather than as a process mediated by aesthetic convention. It is also unhistorical: the critics are describing their personal responses to the picturesque, and confuse those responses with meanings that were available to viewers at the time.

COMPANY PAINTING

The capture of Agra by British forces in 1803 made the Taj more accessible to European visitors and stimulated a demand for images that English artists alone could not meet. Indian artists were swift to adapt their style to appeal to the tastes of the new clientele, thus giving rise to a new genre of so-called 'Company' painting.

That term is used in general for any works produced in the late eighteenth or early nineteenth century by Indian artists for Western patrons (especially for employees of the East India Company – hence the term). Initially, a number of artists had migrated to Calcutta and begun to produce natural history drawings – images of India's flora and fauna – either for individual connoisseurs or for scientific institutions such as the city's Botanical Gardens. Typically these were executed in watercolour on English paper. The range of subjects now expanded to include the masterpieces of Mughal architecture. Early patrons often engaged directly and personally with the artists, commissioning views of favourite buildings or decorative elements: a view of the Taj perhaps, or a detail of its pietra dura decoration. Later, as the trade grew, artists could produce ready-made sets of drawings, confident of achieving a sale to one of the increasing number of foreign visitors.

20. West side of the Taj Mahal (i.e. seen from the mosque);
watercolour by an Agra artist, *c.* 1808.

To appeal more successfully to Western tastes, the artists employed single-point perspective in their architectural views, conscious that otherwise Europeans would regard their work as 'incorrect' or naïve. The speed and thoroughness with which they mastered the technique of perspective drawing is one of the unsolved mysteries of Indian art, though it is perhaps no more than a further testament to Indian artists' long-established ability to assimilate and adapt. Images of the Taj typically show it obliquely and include details such as the geometrical paving of the terrace with a mastery of recession that is startling. Their accuracy in the depiction of the building's forms – including the notoriously difficult dome – surpasses that found in most European artists' work of the period.

What at first they left out, which their European rivals always included, was the foliage of the garden. In the earlier Company images, the building is shown detached, as if floating in space. Perspective apparently could be accomplished without trouble, but the idea of the picturesque – the notion that a building was incomplete without some sign of its natural setting – was seemingly inadmissible. This cannot be explained as signalling an aversion to the English aesthetic, because the building's relation to the garden and the river were, after all, part of the Mughal conception. It arose probably in part from the artists' desire to be scientifically accurate with regard to the building's surfaces, and the consequent need to exclude any potentially distracting element. One of the few named exponents of this early form of the genre was an artist known as Latif. Examples of his work survive in the British Library and in private collections, and there must have been others: the traveller Fanny Parks is one amongst many who claims to have bought some.

21. Taj Mahal; watercolour by Sita Ram for the
Governor General, the Marquis of Hastings, *c.* 1815.

Prefiguring the later phase of the genre, which responds more directly to the picturesque, is the work of the recently rediscovered Bengali artist Sita Ram. A versatile painter, he was engaged by the Marquis of Hastings (Governor General from 1813 to 1823) to accompany his retinue on a tour across northern India, which reached Agra in 1815. When not engaged in breaking up the *hammam* in the fort, Hastings was evidently sufficiently impressed by Mughal architecture to commission a number of views of the Taj. Sita Ram's subtle treatment of light and his preference for asymmetrical perspectives in these images reveal a thorough assimilation of the English watercolour style. By the middle of the century, most Company images of the Taj are miniature paintings made on ivory, for use as brooches or incorporated into box lids.

TOWARDS NEW IMAGES

Inevitably some people took a jaundiced view of the celebrity that all these images of the Taj helped to promote. One or two of the English Victorian artists express less rapture, reflecting perhaps their awareness of having come lately to a scene that was by now widely known, and their fear of being thought unoriginal. As early as 1839 the amateur artist Emily Eden – sister and companion of the Governor General Lord Auckland – with characteristic irony revised the idea that the Taj exceeds expectations:

> *We came here [to Agra] yesterday and went off the same after-noon to see the Taj, which is quite as beautiful, even more so, than we had expected after all we have heard, and as we have never heard of anything else, that just shows how entirely perfect*

it must be. You must have heard and read enough about it, so I
spare you any more, but it really repays a great deal of the trouble
of the journey.

She did not stop to draw it. A resistance to being swept along
on the tide of popular enthusiasm was expressed more forcefully by the later artist William Simpson, who included Agra
in his first Indian tour of 1859–62. He insisted that India's
earlier Islamic architecture was far superior to anything built
by the Mughals, and denounced the mindless acquiescence
to 'Taj-worship', complaining in particular about the tomb's
'tawdry ornament', which he believed to be the result of
unwarranted European influence.

A return to the earlier passion, coupled with a fresh perspective on the scene, is found in the more ingenuous effu-
sions of Edward Lear, the finest English watercolourist to
work in India. Lear spent just over a year in India travelling as
the guest of the viceroy, Lord Northbrook. He reached Agra
in February 1874 and confided his enthusiasm to his private
journal:

Came to the Taj Mahal; descriptions of this wonderfully lovely
place are simply silly, as no words can describe it at all. What a
garden! What flowers! What gorgeously dressed and be-ringed
women; some of them very good-looking too, and all well clothed
though apparently poor. Men, mostly in white, some with red
shawls, some quite dressed in red, or red-brown; orange, yellow,
scarlet, or purple shawls, or white; effects of colour absolutely
astonishing, the great centre of the picture being ever the vast
glittering ivory-white Taj Mahal, and the accompaniment and
contrast of the dark green cypresses, with the rich yellow green

trees of all sorts! And then the effect of the innumerable flights of
bright green parrots flitting across like live emeralds; and of the
scarlet poincinnias and countless other flowers beaming bright
off the dark green!

It is typical of Lear that his eye should have been distracted from the monument by the life and colours of the garden. 'What can I do here?' he mused: 'Certainly not the architecture' (though he did try).

His comment on the presence of apparently impoverished Indians is a measure of the building's accessibility. William Hodges, nearly a century earlier, had noted only that the Mihman Khana was used for the repose of 'any great personage who might come either on a pilgrimage to the tomb, or to satisfy a well-directed curiosity'. But Thomas Daniell observed that the Taj, 'being a spectacle of the highest celebrity, is visited by persons of all rank, and from all parts'; and Fanny Parks was thrilled to see 'gaily-dressed and most picturesque natives'. Lear for his part considered that the Taj redefined social distinctions: 'Henceforth, let the inhabitants of the world be divided into two classes – them as has seen the Taj Mahal; and them as hasn't.'

Amongst the succession of artists who followed in the decades after Lear, those who were most successful in infusing some originality into their perception include Hercules Brabazon and Albert Goodwin from Britain; Edwin Lord Weeks, Lockwood de Forest and William Congdon from America; and Hiroshi Yoshida from Japan. All of these, however, in one sense looked back to the Daniells by focusing on the building in its landscape setting.

An entirely new conception was realised by the Bengali

artist Abanindranath Tagore (a nephew of the famous poet), whose painting of 1902 entitled *The Passing of Shah Jahan* reconstructed the moment when the imprisoned former emperor makes his final farewell to his grandest creation from a balcony of the fort. With his faithful daughter Jahanara sitting at his feet, the dying Shah Jahan reclines in the foreground, gazing at the Taj on the distant horizon. This work won a medal for the artist when it was exhibited at the Delhi Durbar of 1903 and was hailed – by E. B. Havell amongst others – as a masterpiece of the new Indian art. Though painted in oil on wood, it was seen as a successful revival of the style of Mughal art itself, and surpassing it in the expression of emotion. The image encapsulates and propagates the idea of the dethroned emperor pining away, reflecting on the vanity of power and the endurance of love.

The work of Abanindranath and his followers has generally been seen in the context of the emergence of Indian nationalism. Though the artist himself sometimes resisted this association, his quest for a distinctively Indian aesthetic was part of a deliberate departure from the teaching style of the colonial arts schools. The focus on historical subjects that had been popular amongst British artists might also be seen as a reclaiming of Indian history. This attitude is even more overt in the art of Abdur Rahman Chughtai, who claimed to be descended from architects at the Mughal court and who chose to illustrate Persian literary themes as a form of resistance both to colonialism and to Hindu dominance. Following the Partition of India in 1947, Chughtai moved to Pakistan and is widely regarded as a founder of modern Pakistani art.

Another motive for artists such as Abanindranath and Chughtai to concentrate on the human drama and the history rather than on the architecture is that such topics could not be captured by photography. From the middle of the nineteenth century (even before Lear) the majority of images of the Taj were no longer paintings but photographs. The new medium made a swift entry into India: it was practised by professionals and accomplished amateurs within a few years of its invention in Europe. One of the pioneers in Agra was the officer in charge of the medical college, John Murray, who took numerous photographs of the city's Mughal architecture in the 1850s, published as *Agra and its Vicinity* in 1858. Those who followed him include some of the most successful pioneer photographers of India such as Felice Beato, Samuel Bourne and John Edward Saché.

A comparative study of early photographs of the Taj reveals that certain views quickly became standard and were often repeated. The view from the southern gateway of the garden; the view from the opposite bank of the Yamuna; a partially oblique view from the terrace; and a view from a point on the same bank, east of the Taj, looking back westwards towards it – these were the favourites. The repetition is partly explained by the architecture itself, which seems to invite these perspectives. But the early photographers also sought, consciously or unconsciously, to emulate the artists who had preceded them: the views from across the river by Murray and Beato, for example, recreate the composition first drawn by the Daniells. Later photographers imitated the early ones, so as to produce the images that their customers had come to recognise and expect. Saché in particular modelled many of his compositions on successful images by his predecessors.

The work of the commercial photographers took the place of Company painting. Some photographers published their work in albums and many sold individual prints, often advertising them through catalogues, and these were more easily and cheaply obtained by visitors wanting souvenirs or images for their scrapbooks.

With the introduction of simplified apparatus in the twentieth century, tourists no longer had to rely on the commercial photographers but took their own pictures, a practice which of course continues. There are very few visitors today who do not carry a camera, and the Taj must be a contender for the post of most photographed building in the world. This proliferation in numbers has had the paradoxical effect of restricting further treatment of the subject by professionals. With the exception of the distinguished photographer Raghu Rai, who published a sumptuous volume of views of the monument in 1997, there are now few artists or photographers who even consider attempting a subject that has become so hackneyed. The image of the Taj now belongs in the realm of the personal memento.

FOUR LATE TOMBS

The Taj has been replicated not only in painting and photography: less directly but no less strongly it has been reflected and imitated in architecture too. The earliest of these responses are some later Mughal tombs, for the Taj may represent the high point of Mughal funerary architecture but it does not mark the end of the tradition.

The Bibi-ka-Maqbara in Aurangabad, in central India, is the tomb of Begum Rabia Durani, wife of Aurangzeb, Shah Jahan's usurping son. Built in 1678, just thirty years after the completion of the Taj, it makes clear references to it – with the same white marble cladding (though some surfaces, especially on the interior, are covered in white plaster) and four detached white minarets surrounding it. The similarity is in fact to its disadvantage, for in most respects it is a poor copy and so serves to point up the extraordinary qualities of its model. The main building is much smaller, slimmer and more compact, lacking the perfect proportions of the Taj. However, it does introduce one striking point of originality. On entering the building at the level of the terrace, we do not encounter (as we must expect) a sarcophagus surrounded by an octagonal screen. We are forced to stop abruptly as we approach an enormous octagonal hole in the floor; the floor is in fact no more than a narrow gallery running around the sides of the building from which we look down on the tomb, at ground level, below. The distinction between 'false' and 'real' tomb is eradicated, and we are left only with the actual grave, exposed to the dome above.

This change might be explained as a move in the direction of religious orthodoxy, which dictates an uncovered grave. Aurangzeb's own burial nearly thirty years later (he died in 1707) was in a simple enclosure, without any building, also near Aurangabad. But although we can attribute the location of the Bibi-ka-Maqbara to Aurangzeb – since he founded the city – the building itself was not the commission of an emperor grieving for his wife, but of their son, one of the imperial princes, Azam Shah. Even this point of comparison seems to work in the Bibi-ka-Maqbara's disfavour. The tale here is not one of uxorious passion but of filial duty.

From then until the end of their dynasty, the Mughals lacked the resources to build themselves grand tombs. They were buried either in corners of earlier Mughal tombs, notably that of Humayun, or within the *dargahs* of saints whose teachings they admired. The last magnificent Mughal tomb is not imperial at all, but is actually that of one of their more ambitious courtiers. Abu'l Mansur Khan, known as Safdar Jang, served as governor (*nawab*) of the province of Avadh (later Lucknow) and as prime minister or *vizir* of the empire under Muhammad Shah (r. 1719–48). His tomb in Delhi was built in the early 1750s by his son Shuja-ud-Daulah, who succeeded him in the post in Avadh and established the dynasty of the Nawabs of Lucknow. The design of this building owes more to Humayun's tomb (which is near by) than to the Taj, but it is not a direct imitation of either building so much as a further elaboration of common themes. With its cusped arches and generally more florid and etiolated forms, it has often been described as marking the decline of the tradition, a judgement that arises from the assumption that every artistic tradition *must have* a point of decline, just as every story has an ending.

It is not, however, the end. In Lucknow, the city founded by Safdar Jang's descendants, is the tomb of Zinat Algiya, mother of Nawab Muhammad Ali Shah (r. 1837–42). Standing within the precincts of the Husainabad Imambara, built for the same ruler, this tomb is a scaled-down model of the Taj, and has all the appearance of something in an architectural theme park. This was not the first time that the patrons and architects of Lucknow had resorted to straight imitation for architectural effect. The Dilkusha Palace, one of the country houses built for Nawab Sa'adat Ali Khan (r. 1798–1814), was based on John Vanbrugh's design for Seaton Delaval in Northumberland (as published in Colin Campbell's *Vitruvius Britannicus* of 1725). The slightly later Darshan Vilas, built for Nawab Nasir-ud-din

22. The tomb of John Hessing in the Roman Catholic cemetery, Agra,
c. 1803. Its design was attributed by the nineteenth-century traveller
Fanny Parks to the artist Latif.

Haidar around 1830, has four disparate façades, each imitating a different earlier building in Lucknow, creating a stylistic pick-and-mix. Opinion is divided about the merits of the architecture of Lucknow. Its critics, both past and present, are liable to be censured by those who insist that it be taken seriously. But sometimes its spirit was meant to be playful, drawing on an eclectic medley of landmarks from history, including the Taj Mahal.

Zinat Algiya's tomb was anticipated by another, less faithful model situated in Agra itself, built for the Dutchman John Hessing by his widow. Having served as a soldier for the Dutch East India Company in Ceylon, Hessing arrived in India in 1763. He worked first for the Nizam of Hyderabad and then as a mercenary for the Marathas. At the time of his death in 1803 he was their commandant of the Agra fort, defending it against the assault by Lord Lake. His mini-Taj tomb is made of red sandstone not white marble, is square not octagonal, and has minarets integrated into the body of the building rather than detached. But the reference is still clear, and according to Fanny Parks it was designed by one of the Taj's closest observers, the artist Latif.

Hessing's tomb stands in the Roman Catholic cemetery at Lashkarpur, a northern suburb of Agra, where it has some equally pretentious neighbours. In human terms too, Hessing is in good company. Those who lie buried around him include two other famous mercenaries, Walter Reinhardt and General Perron; some descendants of the Bourbons, the royal family of France; and Geronimo Veroneo, wannabe architect of the Taj.

Having served as an inspiration to some of the Mughals' successors, the Taj was later to be entirely reworked in a British imperial idiom. Standing proudly at the end of the central park or *maidan* in Calcutta, the white marble Victoria Memorial Hall is the nearest thing to an imitation of the Taj amongst British buildings in India. Commissioned by Lord Curzon in February 1901, immediately following the death of Queen Victoria, and completed twenty years later, it has sometimes been called a replica of the Taj. It is hardly that, for its appearance is unmistakably English, but in subtle ways it does pay tribute to the legacy of the Mughals as much as to the more recently departed queen. The reasons for this, and for the references being muted, lie in a story that began in the middle of the preceding century.

Early British buildings in India were almost all built in variants of the neoclassical styles that prevailed in Europe. Allowing only for some adaptation to the climate – through the introduction of verandas, for example – the churches, houses, courtrooms and even barracks of early British India are colonial descendants of the Palladian or Greek Revival buildings of home. But a reconsideration of the purpose and methods of British rule in India that followed the outbreak of the rebellion of 1857 led to a refashioning of imperialism that touched even architecture. The question was, how best to represent the empire architecturally? What was the most appropriate style to present a coherent image to both the empire's rulers and its subjects? Conducted by politicians and by architects themselves, this debate involved a broad range of criteria including cost and climate, but centred on matters of cultural resonance. Proponents of neoclassicism cited its

23. Victoria Memorial Hall, Calcutta, designed by
William Emerson, 1901–21.

established position in India, its suitability to the climate (being derived from the architecture of the warm Mediterranean), but especially the humanist values that it was felt to embody, and which were – it was said – intrinsic to the imperial project. Opposing them were partisans for Gothic, who pointed out that classicism by origin was pagan and that a British empire could best express itself through buildings that were demonstrably Christian, since Christian values were the underpinnings of the empire itself.

A third group rejected both solutions and both propositions. The essential character of the British Raj, they insisted, was that it was Indian. British rule flourished because of its ability to identify with the interests of the people, and its architecture should also therefore be Indian. This should not be hard to achieve. Neoclassical and Gothic architecture, after all, were really recreations of historical styles of Europe, and it should be possible to create a new approach that would be similarly based on India's own historical styles. This new approach would be called 'Indo-Saracenic', after the term coined by art historians such as Fergusson to describe Mughal architecture, because the idea was to continue the development of Indian architecture where the Mughals had left off.

The three-sided debate was never settled, not least because the underlying dispute about the motives and nature of British rule was itself not resolved. Its intended outcome was consistency, but the actual outcome was eclecticism, as the proponents of each answer repeatedly sought to demonstrate the efficacy of their preferred choice by example. India therefore contains a large number of fine neoclassical and Gothic buildings, but also a substantial number of 'Indo-Saracenic' ones, designed by British architects who had

24. St John's College, Agra, designed by Samuel Swinton Jacob in 1914, and typical of his 'Indo-Saracenic' mode.

first studied Indian architecture and then sought to apply its forms and adapt its principles to the new requirements of the Raj, by building Indian-style colleges and hospitals, maharajas' palaces and railway stations.

An example that can be seen in Agra itself is St John's College, designed in 1914 by Samuel Swinton Jacob. It is a red sandstone affair, with great arched portals and a skyline that is capped by domes and *chhatris*. Jacob has been seen as a leading practitioner of the movement. He spent most of his career in Jaipur, the capital of a semi-independent princely state, where he worked in close collaboration with Indian colleagues who helped him develop his expertise. As a result, some of his work is in fact much more convincingly Indian than the pastiches that passed for such in cities under direct British rule, including Agra.

Another exponent was William Emerson. A pupil of the Gothicist William Burges, Emerson first went to India in 1864, at the start of his career, and designed the Crawford Market in Bombay in a style of which his teacher would have approved. But in two subsequent works – Muir College in Allahabad and a hospital in Bhavnagar in Gujarat – he attempted to adapt Indian styles. He did not pretend that they were authentic, and wisely chose to defend them by celebrating hybridity, citing St Mark's in Venice as the exemplar of such an approach in Europe. The Indo-Saracenic, he said, 'carries out the idea of showing the influence of the British Raj on modern Indian buildings'.

Back in Britain in 1870, he gave a lecture to the Royal Institute of British Architects, selecting as his topic the greatest of Indian buildings, the Taj Mahal. He carefully skirted any academic issues: unsure on the question of Western involvement in its design, he pronounced it possible but unnecessary. The lecture is mostly a panegyric. He calls the Taj 'a more beautiful place than I ever dreamed of ... a place in which a cold-blooded Caucasian can perhaps realise somewhat the poetical and luxurious feeling of the voluptuous Easterns'. His practice in Britain did not flourish as he might have hoped, and he opted instead for official roles in the profession, becoming president of RIBA in 1899.

When Lord Curzon, as viceroy, proposed the construction of a memorial to Victoria in Calcutta, the capital of her empire in India, he selected Emerson as the most suitable architect on the basis of his previous experience in India and the eminence of his office. He most certainly did not want an Indo-Saracenicist. Curzon was an ardent admirer of Indian architecture and (as we shall see in the next chapter) did more than anyone else in his generation to promote the conservation of historic monuments, including the Taj; but he was as firm in his conviction that new buildings constructed for the Raj should be neoclassical. What he demanded from Emerson for this project was 'the Italian Renaissance style'. As he later reasoned:

> *In Calcutta – a city of European origin and construction – where all the main buildings had been erected in a quasi-classical or Palladian style, and which possessed no indigenous architectural type of its own – it was impossible to erect a building in any native style. A Moghul building ... would have been ridiculous in the commercial and official capital of India, and quite unsuited for the memorial of a British Sovereign. A Hindu fabric would have been profoundly ill adapted for the purposes of an exhibition. It was self-evident that a structure in some variety of the*

*classical or Renaissance style was essential, and that a European
architect must be employed.*

Anyone looking at the building as constructed might rea-
sonably conclude that he got pretty much what he asked for.
To be pedantic, it is perhaps less Italian Renaissance than
English Baroque, as the main dome recalls St Paul's, but
either way it is decidedly classical European. Curzon was
more than satisfied.

And yet there is a haunting shadow of the Taj about the
building, suggesting that the architect had not forgotten his
youthful passion and was bold enough to subvert the patron's
plan. The influence of the Taj announces its presence chiefly
in the main material: the same white marble from Makrana.
There is a more subtle echo in the composition: the large
central dome rises over an arched portal and is surrounded
both by smaller domes over *chhatris* and by towers with yet
smaller domes (which have a pronounced Mughal profile),
and the whole stands on a terrace overlooking a formal garden
set with water bodies. The language, to be sure, is English,
but it has the air of something translated, of conveying something that began as Indian, and one might be forgiven for
wondering just which empress is here being honoured.

A TAJ IN THE GARDEN

Whilst Emerson was preparing his subversive plans, a now
neglected scholar named Edmund Smith was hard at work
in Agra studying the Mughal buildings. His approach did not
require historical research into documents and records, but
the meticulous drawing of architectural details, which were

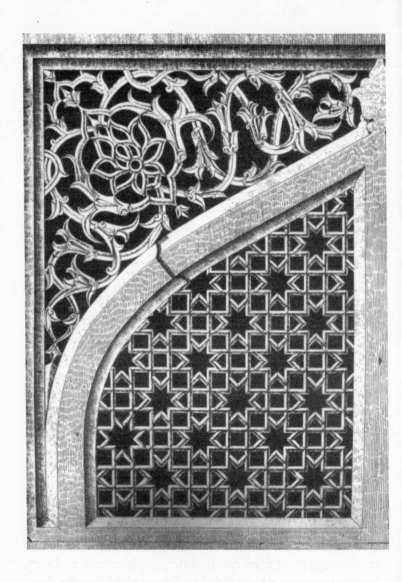

25. Part of the screen in the veranda of the tomb of Sheikh Salim Chishti at Fatehpur Sikri, as drawn by Edmund Smith, 1896.

then published to inspire students at art schools and technical colleges. Smith produced volumes covering the buildings of Fatehpur Sikri and Sikandra, and colour decoration in Agra, and some of his plates were also published in an annual known as the 'Technical Art Series', a loose-leaf portfolio that was intended for use by designers. At the same time Constance Villiers-Stuart wrote a book and some articles for *Country Life* on Mughal gardens. Her approach was more narrative than visual, and in places her writing is somewhat romantic – she gives a very colourful account of the meeting and marriage of Jahangir and Nur Jahan – but she also had some original insights into how the gardens were used.

Sources such as these were instrumental in first persuading and then helping Edwin Lutyens to include a Mughal garden in the design of Viceroy's House. Lutyens, as we have seen, was hostile to any suggestion from politicians that he should make the architecture Indian, to appease local sentiment. In exasperation he argued, 'God did not make the Eastern rainbow pointed, to show his wide sympathies.' The efforts of the Indo-Saracenic architects he thought ridiculous and saw them as sufficient reason not to pursue the attempt; he also derided the work of Swinton Jacob, who at the outset was briefly appointed as his unwanted adviser.

But having registered his protest, Lutyens conceded the point and searched for Indian forms that could be admitted without detracting from his sternly Roman imperial scheme. As a result, the design of Viceroy's House includes some wonderfully transfigured Indian elements, notably the dome and its drum, derived from the Buddhist *stupa* at Sanchi. In the garden he was more playful. The fountains and water channels, pergolas and flower beds, do not replicate the forms of any particular Mughal garden but teasingly allude to them in the fashioning of something new. The garden is spread out before the looming rear façade of the former palace, much like the garden of the Taj beneath an equally imposing dome. It is a strange tribute from a die-hard imperialist to the magic that he tried so staunchly to resist.

Later architectural references to the Taj, though perhaps more sincerely felt, are also less successful. Just outside Agra (on the right of the road as you approach from Delhi) stands a brand-new temple erected in honour of a local spiritual leader known as Guru Dev, which purports to be a replica of the Taj. It is certainly domed and has flanking minarets, but it looks as though it is made of soap. If you admire the Taj it would be best to avert your eyes; it will only make you angry.

Within Agra itself the legacy of the Taj survives in the trade in carved scale models and in the continuing (or rather revived) craft of pietra dura inlay. The city contains countless emporia stacked high with marble objects of various kinds – from candlesticks and coasters to chessboards and even furniture – all decorated with inlaid semi-precious stones set in floral designs that dimly echo those in the Taj. Behind each shop is a studio where you can watch the craftsmen at work. They are not hard to find, indeed you will be hard pressed to prevent your taxi-driver from taking you to one. And so, if you choose and can pay the price, you can take home the semblance of a piece of the Taj, as a marble box or a flower vase, or a table-top for your garden.

5

....

TO HAVE AND TO HOLD

In 2007 people across the world voted via internet and mobile phone for the 'New Seven Wonders of the World'. Philon of Byzantium's original list has become somewhat depleted (as only the Egyptian pyramids survive), and a Swiss-based organisation engaged the popular imagination in finding replacements. A publicity campaign in India ensured that the Taj was amongst the successful candidates. According to one newspaper report, eighteen million votes for the Taj were sent via the internet and a further twelve million by SMS text message. It was assumed that the majority of these thirty million votes were cast by patriotic Indians, rather than by fair-minded Americans or disinterested French, and that India had therefore 'done itself proud'.

Following the announcement of the result one headline read: 'The Message Rings Loud – You Just Can't Count India Out!' There is a possible confusion here. Is the source of pride the strength of the case for the Taj's inclusion in the top seven or the fact that so many Indians have access to computers and mobile phones? Or are these two things in some mysterious way connected? Both might be seen as examples in their different ways of what commentators like to call India's 'soft power' – a phrase which itself carries a hint of computer jargon whilst referring to the country's ability to command cultural and political respect.

India's self-image has changed in recent decades in ways that stress its development and rely less on its heritage. But the indispensable Taj is carried forward into the world of the SMS. The New Seven Wonders episode illustrates the Taj's role in modern Indian cultural politics. But that role is not new: it was established by a British viceroy a century ago. It was Curzon who first declared it a national monument and insisted that its maintenance was the responsibility of the government of India. Its conservation and its modern political meanings have been entwined ever since.

THE LIGHT OF CURZON

George Nathaniel Curzon was appointed Viceroy of India in 1899, at the age of thirty-nine, largely on the strength of his own recommendation. Fearful that no one else would think of it, he proposed his own candidacy, pointing out that having served as Parliamentary Under-Secretary for India from 1891 he was conversant with Indian affairs, and he had visited the subcontinent a number of times.

Political historians do not generally rate his rule as viceroy a success. The period was marked by his disastrous partition of Bengal (an act that was later embarrassingly reversed), and he had to resign in 1905, half-way through his second term, having quarrelled with his commander-in-chief, Lord Kitchener. Despite all this, he is regarded with respect by many who are interested in architecture or in conservation, because of the efforts that he made to preserve India's forests, wildlife and architectural heritage. The last of these in particular he made central to government policy, urging that the maintenance of ancient monuments was a 'sacred trust', and a part of the duty of imperial rule. In ringing tones, he declared:

> I regard the stately or beautiful or historic fabrics of a bygone age, independently of the purposes for which they were set up, or the faith for which they were dedicated, as a priceless heirloom, to be tenderly and almost religiously guarded by succeeding generations; and during my administration of the Government of India no one shall find me niggardly or grudging in the practical realization of this aim. We are not ordinarily so rich in originality ourselves as to afford to allow the memorials of an earlier and superior art or architecture to fall into ruin; and I accept the conservation of the ancient monuments of India as an elementary obligation of Government.

To a large extent, he attended to this matter personally. There can rarely have been a statesman so well educated in architectural history and contemporary design, and when travelling around the country he made it a point to visit historic sites and offer advice about conservation techniques, something previously unheard of amongst the duties of a viceroy. He organised and personally supervised the restoration of many buildings that were under direct British control, including the Mughal buildings of Delhi and Agra, and he urged maharajas, temple trusts and other private owners to take similar steps for buildings under their charge. His speeches are littered with references to both old and new buildings in whichever place his duties took him. When opening a new college or hospital in a provincial town or a princely state, he would invariably comment not only on the building's purpose and its expected benefits to society, but on its design and its relation to the historic architecture of the region.

Though it must have dismayed some of his political aides, his passion for architecture became legendary so that, when he went on tour, buildings were hurriedly restored for his inspection and gratification. Sometimes too hurriedly. A disaster occurred at Mount Abu in Rajasthan, where the white marble Jain temples were whitewashed in his honour and Curzon, far from being delighted as his hosts had planned, delivered an impromptu lecture on the proper methods of conservation. Amongst his more successful interventions was the return from the South Kensington Museum of the pietra dura plaques that had been removed from the Hall of Audience in the Red Fort in Delhi. These attractive pieces had been looted after the suppression of the rebellion in 1857 and were later sold to the British government. Curzon arranged for them to be put back where they belong.

He did not always work alone and perhaps his single most important legacy was to give proper prestige and funding to the Archaeological Survey of India. This organisation had been established under the government of India back in the 1860s by General Alexander Cunningham, a soldier turned archaeologist. In its first few decades it depended entirely on the efforts of Cunningham and a few assistants and successors such as H. B. W. Garrick and James Burgess. It was wisely called a 'survey' for, such was the limit on their funding, in many historic sites that they toured they could do little more than map the extent of the problem that would face anyone undertaking their conservation. This was the challenge that Curzon took up. In 1902 he appointed the young archaeologist John Marshall as director general of the ASI, ensured

26. The throne of the Hall of Audience in the Red Fort in Delhi. The dark panels on the wall behind are pietra dura plaques, looted in 1857 and replaced by Curzon in 1903.

that he had adequate funds and staff to initiate restoration as well as surveying, and helped draw up the necessary legislation to protect ancient monuments from the depredations of vandals and developers. Marshall long outlasted Curzon in office and is still revered by many as one of the founders of modern Indian archaeology; and their legislation is still in force.

Pride of place in Curzon's view of Indian architecture was occupied – of course – by the Taj Mahal. He saw it on his first visit to India in 1887 and fell in love immediately with 'the pearl of fabrics, the gem of man's handiwork, the most devotional of temples, the most solemn of sepulchres, the peerless and incomparable Taj'. He described it as 'designed and finished like a jewel, a snow-white emanation starting from a bed of cypresses and backed by a turquoise sky, pure, perfect and unutterably lovely'.

Only two and half centuries old in Curzon's time, the Taj was better preserved than many ancient and dilapidated temples; but its beauty and fame earned it priority in his conservation plan, and it plainly needed some attention. Over a century before, the artist William Hodges recorded that the fountains were in 'tolerable repair' and functioning, that the garden was 'still kept in decent order', and that the tomb itself was 'in a perfect state', but that all the other buildings of the complex bore 'strong marks of decay'. A little later Thomas Daniell noted the absence from the pietra dura panels of stones that had reportedly been prised out by Jats and Marathas, and Curzon himself noted that this dishonourable tradition had been continued in the early nineteenth century by the British, whilst enjoying their tiffin and quadrilles.

On the other hand, some efforts to replace missing or

decayed pieces of stone facing had been made in 1811 and again in 1864. This led the art historian James Fergusson to comment in 1876 that the Taj 'has been fortunate in attracting the attention of the English, who have paid sedulous attention to it for some time past'. Fergusson was not here being partisan towards his compatriots, for he was bitter and scornful about the treatment of the Red Fort in Delhi in the aftermath of the 1857 rebellion, where colonnades and whole buildings had been needlessly demolished on the pretext of making the fort indefensible in future, but in reality as an act of vengeance and spite. The Taj had mercifully been spared such treatment, but there was still work to be done. In particular, Fergusson recognised that the heavily overgrown condition of the garden, though pleasing to an English picturesque sensibility, was not what the Mughals had intended: 'The long rows of cypresses ... backed up by masses of ever-green foliage, lend a charm to the whole which the founder and his children could hardly have realised.'

The pruning and replanting of the garden was a major element in the work commissioned by Curzon, along with the further replacement of missing or decayed stone on the buildings. Recognising that the Taj was a complex and not a single monument, he evicted a busy market from the Jilaukhana, or forecourt, and rebuilt a wall and arcade on its eastern side that had collapsed. Ever attentive to detail, he ordered costumes for the attendants – white tunics and green turbans, which he insisted were authentic Mughal garb – and benches for the garden, including the white marble seats by the central pool that are now used by couples having their photograph taken.

His finishing touch was the metal mosque lamp that hangs in the tomb's central chamber above the sarcophagi. It is agreed that there would originally have been a lamp in this position; indeed the original chain was still in place, but the lamp itself was missing. Unable to find a suitable replacement in India, Curzon wrote to Lord Cromer, then Britain's second secretary in Cairo, asking him to procure one. Curzon remembered admiring lamps in mosques in Cairo during earlier travels, and suggested that one such reproduced in silver would be just the thing. He evidently did not consider that introducing an Egyptian object into a Mughal tomb would be inappropriate, because as he explained to Cromer, 'the style of the Taj you know to be what we call Indo-Saracenic, which is really Arabic, with flowering substituted for geometric patterns'. Unmoved by this lesson in architectural history from so great an expert – or perhaps distracted by matters of state – Cromer failed to deliver and Curzon had to undertake the commission himself. When returning to Britain he stopped at Cairo and ordered what he wanted in person, arranging for it to be sent to India and duly installed.

Curzon's lamp has recently been identified by one influential scholar as a prime example of a 'colonial aesthetic', which is defined as 'an aesthetic of difference, of distance, of subordination, of control'. The idea is that for a viceroy to pronounce on the building's style and historical affiliations, and to determine what ornaments might best suit it, amounts to an Olympian gesture of mastery. It was the fashioning of knowledge to assert power. Along the same lines, others detect an appropriation of authority in the Mughal-style trappings of the Delhi Durbar of 1903, staged by Curzon as a celebration of the accession of Edward VII as King Emperor. Even more broadly, the British recreation of Indo-Saracenic as a movement in colonial architecture has been interpreted as a gesture of mastery, based on Britain's self-accorded right to define and use India's traditions. Invoking cultural theorists such as Michel Foucault and Edward Said, such arguments explore the links between knowledge, visual culture and colonial ideology.

On the other hand, we may question whether there is anything uniquely 'colonial' about appropriations of history. The Mughals themselves assimilated foreign objects and earlier Indian forms into their buildings. The British architects of the Indo-Saracenic movement were at one level applying to India the very same method that other architects of the time adopted in their approach to Europe's own historical architecture. In its treatment of precedent, Indo-Saracenic architecture is the counterpart of the Greek and Gothic revivals – movements that certainly exude confidence, but which are at the same time grounded in respect for a past that was deemed greater, and worthy of emulation. In any event, Curzon was not amongst the advocates of Indo-Saracenic, preferring a Renaissance style for imperial buildings, as we have seen in the case of the Victoria Memorial Hall. The colonial aesthetic, if such a thing existed, was neither unified nor consistent.

At the time the objection that was raised concerned a rather different aspect of Curzon's claim to authority. He was inspired in part by the Society for the Protection of Ancient Buildings, founded in Britain in 1877 by William Morris, but he departed from their guiding principles in one crucial respect. For whilst the SPAB decried any 'misplaced enthusiasm' which led to the replacement of missing features, Curzon merrily recreated whatever had been removed. Quite apart from the semi-precious stones that had been gouged out of the cenotaphs in the Taj by early-nineteenth-century

27. The gate of Akbar's tomb at Sikandra; watercolour by an artist of Agra, *c.* 1808. The artist, like Curzon later, evidently felt that the minarets should be completed: at the time the painting was made the crowning pavilions were in fact missing.

picnickers, this policy led him to replace the missing balustrade on Itimad-ud-Daulah's tomb, and the kiosks or *chhatris* on top of the minarets on the gateway of Akbar's tomb at Sikandra. Whilst many believed that these *chhatris* had been blown off by trigger-happy Jats, some questioned whether they had ever been completed in the first place. Curzon responded to both groups by pointing out what was incontrovertible: there were no *chhatris* now, and the broken or unfinished stumps cannot represent the architect's intention. The design of his replacements, however, was little more than informed guesswork.

During the restoration of the Hall of Audience in the Agra fort, a question arose as to whether to replace the white plaster covering the sandstone columns. Some suggested that this plaster was a later addition and it would be more authentic to remove it altogether. Curzon asserted that whatever the date of the existing plaster, the original intention must have been to have a plaster covering, and so it should be replaced. The slightly rough surface of the columns underneath his layer of plaster indicates that he was almost certainly correct.

As such episodes illustrate, Curzon was not one to spend a long time reflecting on the limits of his authority. He was confident that his restoration work at the Taj was appreciated by Indians, even more than by Europeans, that such work brought Indians and British closer together and that 'no co-operation of this description is to be despised'. He also had in mind its place in preserving his name for posterity. As he once wrote to his wife from Agra: 'If I had never done anything else in India, I have written my name here, and the letters are a living joy.' A superior sort of graffiti, perhaps. But if there is a hint of vanity in his claim, even his critics must concede that his work at the Taj was both beneficial and timely.

OWNERSHIP AND CARE

Through the course of the twentieth century the status of the Taj continued to rise in both national and international awareness. Foreigners visit India in ever increasing numbers and a higher proportion of Indians travel around their own country; and for both groups the Taj is a major attraction, eagerly reported on to those who have stayed behind but who might plan a visit in another year. A century on from Curzon, the Taj is not only a building of unrivalled prestige, it is also a major source of revenue, through ticket sales and souvenirs. The Taj receives on average eight thousand visitors per day, which amounts to nearly three million a year (placing it, for the sake of comparison, not far behind the Sistine Chapel in Rome).

In this context it is not surprising – indeed it is healthy – that there should be continuous debate and argument over its proper maintenance and care. At issue are not only per-ceived or real threats to the building's fabric, but also the best responses to those threats. There is also the question of who should be its proper custodians. Who is ultimately responsi-ble for it: politicians, as the people's elected representatives, or expert archaeologists, as members of the government body (the ASI) specifically charged with the care of historic monu-ments? Members of these two groups can be in conflict, pulled by competing interests. For example, if archaeologists identify a local industry as a potentially damaging pollutant, they may have to call on the politicians to take the unpopular step of closing it down. Conversely, politicians might wish to use the monument to stage a popular event that would enhance their own prestige, but run up against cautious objections from archaeologists. Who, then, has greater authority is not always clear, as members of both groups tend to claim power and deny accountability with equal vigour.

In the context of this sometimes incapacitating confusion, the local Waqf board has recently advanced a claim to custodianship, and is preparing to bring its case to court. Common in the Islamic world, Waqf boards are charitable organisations which typically own and maintain great buildings. A major mosque, for example, might have such a board as part of its institutional foundation, responsible for managing the letting of its outbuildings or other properties for commercial purposes, and using the revenue to support the mosque's teaching and charitable functions and to maintain its fabric. Waqf records, where preserved, are often used by architectural historians trying to reconstruct a major building's institutional history. As it happens, there are no known Waqf records relating to the Taj, but (as explored earlier in this book) the Taj complex was evidently intended to function as an economic entity – deriving income from the connected caravanserais, from the villages with which it was endowed, and perhaps even from the produce of the garden – and there must logically have been a body in charge of this.

On this or some such ground (the ground and the reasoning are in truth not entirely clear) the Sunni Waqf board of Uttar Pradesh, the modern state in which Agra is situated, has made its claim. Their lawyers are no doubt privately refining the argument, but meanwhile the public expressions of the board's spokesmen, as reported in the press, fail to convince, and indicate a lack of familiarity with the handling of documentary sources. The chairman of the board, for example, was reported in March 2005 as saying: 'We have copies of Shah Jahan's original will stored in the London Museum, and other documentation that proves the Taj is Waqf property. Shah Jahan himself writes in his will that the Taj be handed over to Waqf after his death.' Historians might wonder what document is here being referred to – or, for that matter, what the 'London Museum' is (surely not the Museum of London, which is dedicated to the history of that city). A scholarly edition of the Persian text of the *Padshahnama* (the official history of Shah Jahan's reign) was published as a printed book in 1866–72; copies of this book can be found in many libraries, including of course the British Library, which before its move to the Euston Road was formerly housed in the same building as the British Museum – a museum *in* London. So perhaps this is the text referred to. But it is not a will, and it certainly does not say that the Taj is Waqf property.

Another argument is that the Taj is 'Waqf-by-use'. Citing past rulings of India's Supreme Court that any building in continuous use for religious purposes can be so deemed, the Waqf board argues that the original annual Urs ceremony in memory of Mumtaz Mahal, and the regular holding of Friday prayers in the mosque of the complex that continues even in the present day, qualify the Taj for this status. But these have not been the buildings' only uses historically, and it will be up to the court to clarify whether 'continuous use' also covers partial or occasional use.

The legal move from the Waqf board has prompted counter claims from organisations such as the Bajrang Dal that operate in the name of Hinduism. They see the Waqf claim as a form of Muslim self-assertion, and their opposition is intended to draw the Taj into an area of modern religious conflict. Taking their cue from the far-fetched theories of P. N. Oak, they proclaim the building's supposed origin as a Hindu temple built by Raja Jai Singh or his forebears and insist on its being renamed 'Tejo Mai Mahal' if not actually re-converted into a temple. There is also a rival claim from a Shia Waqf board on the ground that Mumtaz Mahal, like her father, was a member of the Shia faith.

People in the public eye who have responded to invitations to comment on these various claims have mostly been briskly dismissive. The celebrated lyricist and Urdu poet Javed Akhtar has been quoted as saying, 'All these so-called religious organisations should go fly a kite. Their claims are utter rubbish.' The advertising guru Suhel Seth has remarked, 'Shah Jahan bequeathed the Taj to all Indians and not to a pack of jokers. All these claims are bizarre.' Most such responses stress the idea of the Taj as common heritage, belonging to Muslims and Hindus equally, with some pointing out that it was built by both Muslim and Hindu craftsmen in the first place. For some, the inheritance is even wider: the Taj belongs to humanity.

The Archaeological Survey of India, whose custodianship the claims directly challenge, has responded publicly by declaring that none of them can be substantiated because 'the Taj Mahal is a national monument'. Perhaps fearing that such rhetoric will be less persuasive than the language of bureaucracy, they add that they are charged with its maintenance 'under section 3 subsection 1 of the Ancient Monument Preservation Act of 1904' – a reference to the law enacted by Curzon. In the course of legal argument no doubt someone

28. Two cartoons by Jug Suraiya and Ajit Ninan. The first was prompted by a ruling by India's Supreme Court in the autumn of 2006, enforcing the zoning laws; the second records the model of the Taj on the Thames in 2007.

will ask how a British viceroy assumed the right to determine its ownership, but in the longer term none of these partisan claims is likely to prove sustainable. The courts are bound by the 'secular' values of the constitution; and even those politicians who question such values still need to court votes from all communities. For everyone, there is too much at stake.

In the meantime the arguments have focused attention again on the monument's state of repair. Even the wildest claim is given some edge by the apparent failings in its current maintenance (though it may be doubted whether any of the claimants would be equipped to take better care of it). Concerns about pollution damaging the surface of the marble have been partially resolved through the forcible closure of some local industries (to the inevitable disgruntlement of local residents) and the exclusion of vehicles from a protective zone around the complex. But UNESCO's World Heritage Committee, which nominates and then monitors the condition of World Heritage Sites, is reported to be still unhappy about the cleanliness of the surrounding area and particularly of the river, and has called for a larger buffer zone. Agra is home to two designated UNESCO sites (the Taj and the fort), with a third (Fatehpur Sikri) near by, and it rankles with the Ministry of Tourism of the central government that they cannot on the strength of this apply for Agra itself to be designated as a World Heritage City. UNESCO has rebuffed any such suggestion by pointing to the city's dilapidated condition and the failure to preserve its original urban fabric. The historic monuments – the designated ones and a handful of others – survive as isolated pockets in a modern provincial city that one has to admit is fairly miserable by current Indian standards.

During the 'Taj Mahotsav' celebrations held in September 2005 to commemorate the building's alleged 350th anniversary, the state government of Uttar Pradesh asked the ASI for permission to floodlight it, so that it could serve as a splendid backdrop for a concert. The ASI refused, arguing that during an earlier illumination that went ahead (for a concert by Yanni) 'millions of insects were drawn towards the shining white marble of the Taj. Their excreta is feared to contain chemicals that could corrode the marble and damage the monument.' They also complained that during the opening ceremony for the Taj Mahotsav itself, vehicles – presumably cars of politicians – were driven into the fort, and generators spewed out fumes. There was similar concern in 2006 over a proposal to use the Taj as the venue for a concert in support of AIDS victims, whose star billing was to include the Puerto Rican singer Ricky Martin. Sometimes it is safer to express reservations in terms of local sensibilities rather than complex matters of conservation and insect life: on this occasion an ASI officer commented that the plan was absurd because the people of Agra have no idea who Ricky Martin is.

Behind the headlines the arguments are not all political, and there is continuing discussion about conservation policies and techniques. There was a recent proposal, for example, to clean the marble surface by using *multani mitti* – a natural clay face-pack treatment that has been used for centuries by Indian women – adding a further dimension to the feminisation of the Taj. Curzon's defiance of SPAB principles established a norm that remains in force: parts of the stone facing of the buildings that have been damaged or corroded by pollution or weather are still regularly replaced. Curzon had argued that this approach was appropriate in India, where one could still find suitably skilled craftsmen to carry out the work. Thanks in part to the continuing policies and the patronage of the ASI this remains true today, and at prominent sites under ASI control one frequently encounters craftsmen, hunched over a slab of stone, carving a moulding, as if construction were still ongoing.

A CORRIDOR OF POWER

In 2002 a plan was drawn up to develop a chain of tourist facilities and commercial outlets along the line of the river bed between the Taj and the fort. The two monuments were to be linked by a serpentine structure that would cost an estimated Rs 175 *crore* (roughly US$40 million), and was to be known as the 'Taj Heritage Corridor'. The chief minister of Uttar Pradesh at this time was Mayawati, the leader of the regionally based Bahujan Samaj Party. It is generally assumed that the scheme had her blessing. Certainly the plans were approved and work began without the central government or the ASI being consulted, or even becoming aware. As soon as the rapidly advancing construction was brought to their somnolent attention they sat up and objected, and a court injunction halted further progress.

There was also a public outcry. The sheer tastelessness of the idea, if it did not leave one speechless, was ground for vehement objection. Agra is already grim enough without the intrusion of a modern monstrosity in its historic core, and how could anyone be so insensitive as to propose building next door to India's most famous and beautiful monument? The cynical reply was not long in coming. The revenue to be derived from such a scheme by building contractors and the kick-backs to their political patrons would be enormous. Amongst many Indian voters there is a resigned expectation that at least some politicians will be venal. But there is also a class dimension. Mayawati's power base rests on large numbers of underprivileged members of the 'scheduled castes', many of whom might be supposed (by those who have had better opportunities in education) to regard history and aesthetics with indifference. Some political foot-soldiers might even be expected to view such actions with admiration, feeling that politicians enhance their prestige by showing what they can get away with, in defiance of higher authorities, and in striking a blow against privilege.

There is a common problem with great monuments. The assumption that local people always benefit from their proximity to something that is universally admired – as a source of tourist revenue and related business – is not always shared by local people themselves, who may complain that its presence, and regulations concerning its care, place restrictions on them, for example by limiting the range of other businesses that they might wish to develop. They might not share a sense of the importance of preserving it, regarding it instead as a local resource to be exploited only for as long as it lasts. One sometimes hears residents of Agra insisting that the city would be a better place without the Taj. It is hard to agree, but one can understand their vexation.

The sense of outrage against Mayawati – the feeling that either she or some of her officials put in jeopardy a priceless national treasure – comes mainly from educated middle-class city-dwellers, who are not amongst her constituents. Her now aborted scheme has in no way diminished her in the eyes of her supporters. For a while she lost her hold on office, but not because of the Taj scandal, and she was later re-elected having successfully broadened her power base to include members of the higher castes. Legal action against her was stalled, as the central police authority, the CBI, declared that their legal advisers were against pursuing the matter. Some commentators scent political intervention here, as Mayawati had proved herself to be an expedient ally of the Congress-led coalition forming the central government in Delhi. The Supreme Court announced itself dissatisfied with the CBI response.

Quite apart from political and legal issues, larger questions remain about the physical damage done. The work that had been carried out before the halt was called had involved 2.25 million cubic metres of earth-filling, 45,000 cubic metres of stone-work and 2,000 cubic metres of concrete (at a cost of Rs 200 million). Concrete foundations for the buildings had been sunk into the river bed, diverting the flow of the water and raising concerns about the possible impact on the foundations of the Taj itself. There have always been differing views about the structure and stability of the Taj's foundations. They are described in Lahauri's *Padshahnama*, but they cannot now be fully understood without a recklessly intrusive survey, and cautious opinion has therefore favoured leaving them well alone. What damage has already been inflicted by tipping such vast quantities of stone and concrete into the river cannot be assessed, for fear that the investigation itself might cause yet further harm. The current plan is therefore simply to hide the results of the Taj Corridor adventure by covering it up and planting over the top of it, and developing a surrounding green belt. Even this solution will cost the taxpayer a further Rs 400 million.

Ironically the disastrous scheme appears to have been

inspired at least in part – and quite unwittingly – by proposals submitted by professional conservationists from the USA. The US National Park Service in 1994, and later the Department of Landscape Architecture of the University of Illinois, were both commissioned by the Uttar Pradesh Tourism Department to prepare plans for improving the area around the Taj. The first report, by the Park Service, proposed a vast 'Taj National Park' on the far bank, behind the Mahtab Bagh. The Illinois scheme incorporated this and expanded on it with other green areas around the Mahtab Bagh and the Taj complex, to be called the 'Taj Mahal Cultural Heritage District'. This was in line with what UNESCO has indicated it would like to see. Mostly the plan included great avenues and lawns, along with 'pools, water channels, and trees to bring shade and comfort', but it also included visitor centres with 'spaces for gift shops, audiovisual presentations, tour guide offices, and public facilities'. None of this was implemented as proposed. But it clearly made an impression. Somewhere along the line, someone seems to have seized on the commercial potential suggested in the report. The avenues were axed, and the green 'heritage district' became an exclusively commercial 'heritage corridor'.

BUNTY AND BABLI GET MARRIED

The daily stamp of tourists' feet, and periodic hail storms that chip the marble, are amongst the hazards of normal wear and tear, which at least keep the craftsmen employed. Pollution and threats of commercial exploitation require more subtle and determined vigilance. The latest fear to emerge is from terrorism. More than once the Agra police have been alerted to an alleged plot by al-Qaida to blow up the Taj. So far these have proved to be hoaxes, the work of publicity seekers. In one recently reported case, the letter making the threat was said to be 'written in Hindi, and the writing resembles that of a junior class student'.

The police and other authorities are naturally obliged to take all such stunts seriously. The elaborate security arrangements involve ever increasing numbers of personnel and advancing technology, with video surveillance, electric fences, metal and explosive detectors and the frisking of each individual visitor. Still, this solemn ritual of access does little to diminish visitors' excitement or anticipation of delight, and all the threats to the building, whether real or perceived, have not dimmed its power over people's imagination or changed its well-established meanings.

Its endurance as a symbol of India, and of love, was wryly illustrated by a couple of scenes in a popular Hindi film released in 2005. Entitled *Bunty aur Babli*, the film tells the tale of a couple of charismatic con artists impelled into a life of crime by their professional disappointments. In one scene they arrange to sell the Taj to an unsuspecting American millionaire whose petulant young girlfriend wants to get married there, and nowhere else. 'I can't believe,' says the credulous victim, 'that anyone would actually sell the Taj Mahal.' 'I can't believe,' replies the trickster under his breath, 'that anyone would actually buy it.' When the duped millionaire arrives with his bride to solemnise their marriage they are refused entry. But in another scene, Bunty and Babli stage their own impromptu wedding against the backdrop of the Taj, encircling the sacred fire on a platform by the riverbank. This scene provoked outrage from one zealous conservationist who asked whether the smoke from the fire might have damaged the building.

Life imitates art. In August 2006 there was much embarrassment when security was breached by an American couple who were in the process of conducting a Muslim wedding in the mosque next to the Taj, assisted by a local *qazi*. One feels rather sorry that they were interrupted. They meant no harm, and were acting out in their own lives three and half centuries of accumulated meaning. Surely Mumtaz and Shah Jahan would have understood.

We have seen many accounts of the Taj Mahal in this book, shaped by the intellectual and political forces of their time, and some have seemed pretty outrageous. Assuming that we do not actually destroy the Taj (and perhaps even if we do), future generations will no doubt construct new meanings for it, fed by their own compulsions. So we might wonder how some of *our* accounts of the Taj – like this one – will seem to them.

MAKING A VISIT?

The months between October and March are generally rec-ommended for overseas visitors to northern India, to avoid the excessive heat of the summer and the torrential rains of the monsoon. But the Taj is open all year round and is impressive in any weather or season – indeed it is spectacular when backed by monsoon storm clouds. It is usually open from sunrise to sunset (two traditionally favoured times of day for viewing), and until midnight on the few days before and after each full moon. It is closed to tourists on Fridays. Actually getting in can take a little time, because of the long queues for tickets (there are no timed or advance tickets) and the tight security. To beat the rush it is best to go early in the morning, before the crowds arrive.

Before entering you will be besieged by photographers offering to take your photograph and promising to have it ready and printed before you depart. They are generally as good as their word (and skilled photographers too). The person offering you what looks like a rolled-up bath cap is trying to be helpful: these are thin plastic galoshes that you can wear over your shoes, obviating the need to remove them before climbing the steps to the terrace. The interior of the tomb is often noisy and the atmosphere quite ripe; but it is not to be missed. It is also important to walk around the terrace behind the tomb, to appreciate its relation to the river and the rest of the city. The most pleasant experience is often walking through the garden, which is so large that despite the numbers of visitors one can often find solitude there. The pavilion in the middle of the western side houses a small site museum.

The city's other star attraction is the fort, built by Akbar but with palaces added later by Shah Jahan. The scene of the emperor's house arrest, this is an important part of the story. Though not as well maintained as a monument of this importance deserves, its gardens and apartments do give us some impression of Mughal court life.

Most visitors to Agra come on a day trip from Delhi, 200 km/125 miles to the north. The two cities are connected by air, rail and road. By any of these means it is perfectly feasible to reach Agra by mid-morning, see the Taj, have lunch, visit the fort, squeeze in some shopping and be back in Delhi by midnight. For those who are pressed for time, this may be the only option; but it makes for a long day and requires missing much of what Agra has to offer. Some of the less frequented monuments are hardly less spectacular and allow one to enjoy the architecture away from the pressing crowds.

In particular it is worth spending half a day on the far bank of the Yamuna visiting the tomb of Itimad-ud-Daulah, the nearby Chini ka Rauza and Aram Bagh, and the Mahtab Bagh (the last for the view of the Taj across the river). Akbar's tomb at Sikandra (a northern suburb of the city) is also worth visiting for the splendid, if stylistically eccentric, buildings and for the extensive garden, populated with black buck and long-tailed langur monkeys. Those travelling by car will

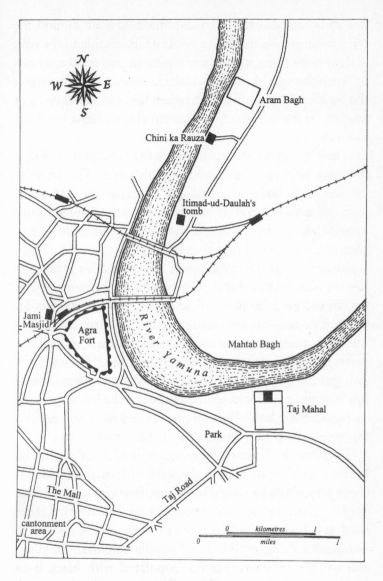

29. Map of Agra.

pass through Sikandra on the road as they approach the city. Akbar's great mosque and palace at Fatehpur Sikri, 40 km/25 miles west of Agra, merit a full day excursion in themselves.

Apart from the monuments, Agra is not an inspiring place. It is a sad fact that India's most beautiful building is located in what has become a dreary city. In its Mughal heyday it must have been magnificent and there are still a few spots where one can catch a glimpse of this. There are picturesque views along the riverbank near the Aram Bagh, for example. But little remains of the old city behind the fort. The elegant mosque built under the patronage of Shah Jahan's daughter Jahanara is sandwiched between the railway line and a shabby market. The old civil lines area of the British era contains some good specimens of colonial bungalows, but these remain in government use and are not accessible. This area was never grand (unlike its counterparts in larger Indian cities established by the British) and it now wears a desolate air.

This explains why comparatively few tourists stay overnight. For those who do, there is a broad range of hotels. Two that are towards the top end are also of architectural merit: the Oberoi group's recently built Amar Vilas (which has an unrivalled view of the Taj) and the Mughal Sheraton, built in the 1970s, which won an Aga Khan award for design.

The former Viceroy's House in New Delhi designed by Edwin Lutyens (now Rashtrapati Bhawan, the official residence of the President of India) can be toured by appointment (applications are best made through a travel agent). Few of the original furnishings and decorations are in place, apart from a stunning Qajar painting of Fath Ali Shah out hunting, on the ceiling of the ballroom, and a collection of British portraits in a small museum in the basement, but a visit is worthwhile for the building alone. The Mughal Gardens behind the palace are open to the public each year for a month, starting around St Valentine's Day. Security is extremely tight (no handbags, mobile phones etc.) and you have to shuffle round on a prescribed route, but it repays the effort, especially for those who are fond of dahlias.

The Victoria Memorial Hall in Calcutta (now Kolkata) has standard museum opening hours (10 a.m. to 4 p.m., closed on Mondays).

FURTHER READING

CHAPTER I

The major sources for Mughal history are the diaries and official histories written or commissioned by the emperors themselves. Most relevant here is the *Padshahnama* written by Abdul Hamid Lahauri and other authors. A full modern translation is still awaited but an edition of the Persian text was published by M. Kabir-ud-Din Ahmad and M. Abd al-Rahim (Calcutta, 1866–72), and translated extracts are included in volume 7 of H. M. Elliot and J. Dowson, *The History of India as Told by Its own Historians* (7 vols, London, 1866–77), and by Wheeler Thackston in Milo Beach and Ebba Koch, *King of the World: The Padshahnama* (London, 1997). The other most relevant Mughal work is the *Tuzuk-i Jahangiri* or *Jahangirnama* (the memoirs of Jahangir). The translation by A. Rogers (2 vols, London, 1909–14) has been superseded by Wheeler Thackston, *The Jahangirnama* (New York, 1999).

For a readable general introduction to Mughal history and courtly culture, Bamber Gascoigne, *The Great Moghuls* (London, 1971) has yet to be beaten, though Annemarie Schimmel, *The Empire of the Great Mughals: History, Art and Culture* (London, 2004) is superb. The story of Nur Jahan and

Jahangir is told in exhaustive detail in Ellison Banks Findly, *Nur Jahan: Empress of Mughal India* (New Delhi, 1993). Diana and Michael Preston, *A Teardrop on the Cheek of Time: The Story of the Taj Mahal* (London, 2007) ventures well beyond the building to give another readable account of the history of the Mughal imperial family. John F. Richards, *The Mughal Empire* (Cambridge, 1993) presents a more sober introduction, focusing on the empire's administrative structure and economy. The substantial output of Irfan Habib includes *An Atlas of the Mughal Empire* (Delhi, 1982), and his edited volume, *Akbar and His India* (Delhi, 1997). For an account of both cohesive and divisive forces driving cultural and intellectual relations between Muslims and Hindus in India, see Aziz Ahmad, *Studies in Islamic Culture in the Indian Environment* (1964; reprinted Delhi, 2000). The classic study of the later Mughal period is Jadunath Sarkar, *Fall of the Mughal Empire* (4 vols, Delhi, 1932–50).

Shah Jahan's famous wine cup now in the V&A is discussed by Robert Skelton, *The Shah Jahan Cup* (London, 1969). François Bernier's *Travels in the Mogul Empire AD 1656–1668* was first published in Paris in 1670; Archibald Constable's translation (1891) was reissued, edited by Vincent Smith (Oxford, 1914). Niccolao Manucci's *Storia do Mogor* was translated by W. Irvine (4 vols, London, 1907–8). Syed Muhammad Latif, *Agra, Historical and Descriptive* (Calcutta, 1896) is also available in modern reprints.

For the decorative arts of the Mughals, see especially two scholarly catalogues: *The Indian Heritage: Court Life and Arts under Mughal Rule*, Victoria & Albert Museum (London, 1982), and Manuel Keene, *Treasury of the World: Jewelled Arts of India in the Age of the Mughals* (London, 2001). Mark

Zebrowski, *Gold, Silver & Bronze from Mughal India* (London, 1997) is a superb study of the metalware.

CHAPTER 2

The outstanding work of architectural history on the Taj is Ebba Koch, *The Complete Taj Mahal and the Riverfront Gardens of Agra* (London, 2006) – which was also remarkably the first scholarly monograph devoted to the building. Two earlier more specialised works remain useful as supplements: Wayne E. Begley and Z. A. Desai, *The Illumined Tomb* (Cambridge, Mass., 1989), which collates all of the contemporary source material relating to the building; and Elizabeth B. Moynihan (ed.), *The Moonlight Garden: New Discoveries at the Taj Mahal* (Washington, 2001), which describes the recent excavation of the Mahtab Bagh. Approaching the monument from the perspective of cultural studies (rather than architecture) is the highly regarded book by Tim Edensor, *Tourists at the Taj* (London, 1998).

General studies of Mughal architecture include Ebba Koch's concise *Mughal Architecture: An Outline of Its History and Development* (Munich, 1991), and her collected essays published as *Mughal Art and Imperial Ideology* (New Delhi, 2001). Catherine B. Asher, *Architecture of Mughal India* (Cambridge, 1992; a volume in the New Cambridge History of India series) provides a good survey and is especially strong on buildings in provincial cities. Also contributing to our understanding of Mughal architecture (focusing on the reign of Akbar) are Michael Brand and Glenn D. Lowry (eds), *Fatehpur Sikri* (Bombay, 1987) and Attilio Petruccioli (ed.), *Fatehpur Sikri* (Berlin, 1992). To relate the Taj and other Mughal buildings to Islamic architecture outside India, a helpful guide is John D. Hoag, *Islamic Architecture* (London, 1975), one of the few surveys of the subject that pays due attention to India. For 'sultanate' or Islamic architecture in India before the Mughals, see part 3 of Christopher Tadgell, *A History of Architecture in India* (London, 1990) and Abha Narain Lambah and Alka Patel (eds), *The Architecture of the Indian Sultanates* (Mumbai, 2006).

Elizabeth Moynihan's study of the *char bagh* is entitled *Paradise as a Garden in Persia and Mughal India* (London, 1982). Sylvia Crowe and Sheila Haywood, *The Gardens of Mughul India* (London, 1972) contains a few outdated views but some good plans and illustrations. Jean-Baptiste Tavernier's *Travels in India*, first published in 1676, was translated by V. Ball and edited by W. Crooke (2 vols, London, 1925). There has as yet been little research on Mughal building methods and processes, but a stimulating essay on this theme is Ahsan Jan Qaisar, *Building Construction in Mughal India* (Delhi, 1988).

CHAPTER 3

The quoted passages by Lahauri, Kalim and Qudsi are amongst those collected by Begley and Desai. Bernier's letter is included in his *Travels*. The Company period memoirs quoted are James Forbes, *Oriental Memoirs* (London, 1813); Major General Sir W. H. Sleeman, *Rambles and Recollections of an Indian Official* (London, 1844; ed. Vincent Smith, London, 1913); Lady Maria Nugent, *A Journal* (London, 1839); Reginald Heber, *Narrative of a Journey through the Upper Provinces of India* (3 vols, London, 1828); and Fanny Parks, *Wanderings of a Pilgrim in Search of the Picturesque* (London, 1850).

James Fergusson's comments are from his *History of Indian and Eastern Architecture* (2 vols, London, 1876). A good account of 'The Veroneo Controversy' is given, under that title, by Jack S. Dixon in *The Journal of Imperial and Commonwealth History* (15/2, 1987). For the views of the main contenders see Vincent Smith, *A History of Fine Art in India and Ceylon* (London, 1911) and E. B. Havell, *Indian Architecture* (London, 1913). Havell is also the author of *A Handbook to Agra and the Taj, Sikandra, Fatehpur-Sikri and the Neighbourhood* (1904; 2nd edn, London, 1912). Vincent Smith, amongst many works, was also a contributor to *The Imperial Gazetteer of India* (26 vols, Oxford, 1908–9), from volume 2 of which is taken his rejection of Indian sculpture as art.

The later opposing definitions of the Taj's style are taken from Gavin Hambly, *Cities of Mughul India* (Toronto, 1968) and R. Nath, *The Immortal Taj Mahal: The Evolution of the Tomb in Mughal Architecture* (Bombay, 1972). In fairness it should be added that Nath is careful to dissociate himself from the views of those such as P. N. Oak, discussed at the end of this chapter. Nath is arguing for Indic inspiration, not a pre-Islamic origin.

The definitive account of the role of Lutyens in the designing of New Delhi is Robert Grant Irving, *Indian Summer: Lutyens, Baker and Imperial Delhi* (New Haven and London, 1981). Many of his views, including his formula for Mughal architecture, are recorded in the biography by his daughter: Mary Lutyens, *Edwin Lutyens* (London, 1980). The clear layout and reliable information of Percy Brown, *Indian Architecture (Islamic Period)* (Bombay, 1942) ensure it a lasting place on the study shelf. Wayne Begley's justly famous if flawed article entitled 'The Myth of the Taj Mahal and a

New Theory of its Symbolic Meaning' is published in *The Art Bulletin* (61, 1979). P. N. Oak's book is also found in a later edition entitled *The Taj Mahal is a Temple Palace* (3rd edn, Delhi, 1974). My previous engagement with it (which elicited the senatorial rebuke) was an article entitled 'Politics and the Taj Mahal', in *Oriental Art* (32/3, 1986). Aldous Huxley's Indian travelogue is *Jesting Pilate* (London, 1926).

CHAPTER 4

There exists a substantial body of work on Mughal painting. Two useful introductory surveys are J. P. Losty, *The Art of the Book in Mughal India* (London, 1982) and J. M. Rogers, *Mughal Miniatures* (London, 1993). Sawai Jai Singh's map of Agra is published in Ebba Koch's *The Complete Taj Mahal*.

The description of the Taj by William Hodges is taken from his *Travels in India* (London, 1793). Hodges's Indian landscapes are the subject of my own book, *The Artificial Empire* (London, 2000), but for a broader study of his work, including that in the South Pacific, see Geoff Quilley and John Bonehill (eds), *William Hodges 1744–1797: The Art of Exploration* (London and New Haven, 2004), a catalogue which accompanied an exhibition held at the National Maritime Museum, London and later at the Yale Center for British Art, New Haven. The comments by the Daniells are taken from the pamphlet accompanying their prints, *Views of the Taje Mahal* (London, 1801). Their Indian travels and aquatints are the subject of Mildred Archer, *Early Views of India* (London, 1980).

Published information about Company painting is dispersed and is mostly found in catalogues of public and private collections and in sale catalogues of dealers and auction houses. Mildred Archer, *Company Painting: Indian Paintings of the British Period* (London, 1992) is the catalogue of the V&A collection, which includes a representative selection of works from Delhi and Agra. The excellent collection in the Oriental and India Office Collections (British Library) is described (but not well illustrated) in Mildred Archer, *Company Paintings in the India Office Library* (London, 1972).

Emily Eden, *Up the Country: Letters from India* (London, 1866) describes her travels with her brother, Lord Auckland. Ray Murphy (ed.), *Edward Lear's Indian Journal* (London, 1953) is the source for Lear's comments. Some of the later artists are discussed in the final chapter of Pratapaditya Pal (ed.), *Romance of the Taj Mahal* (London and Los Angeles, 1989). This book accompanied an exhibition held at the Los Angeles County Museum of Art; the earlier chapters discuss the building and place it in the broader context of Mughal visual and material culture. For the work of Abanindranath Tagore, see especially Partha Mitter, *Art and Nationalism in Colonial India, 1850–1922* (Cambridge, 1994).

Research on photography in India has only recently begun and (as with Company painting) published information is mostly to be found in the catalogues of exhibitions or sales. Maria Antonella Pelizzari (ed.), *Traces of India: Photography, Architecture, and the Politics of Representation, 1850–1900* (Montreal and New Haven, 2003) has excellent coverage, despite thrashing a heavy doctrinal stick throughout. Better at relating photography to other forms of representation such as English landscape and Company painting (indeed, providing a balanced introduction to all three genres) is Pratapaditya Pal and Vidya Dehejia, *From Merchants to Emperors: British*

Artists and India, 1757–1930 (New York and London, 1986), based on the since-dispersed Paul Walter Collection.

The most recent work on the architecture of Lucknow is assembled in Rosie Llewellyn Jones (ed.), *Lucknow: City of Illusion* (New Delhi, 2006). The opening chapters of Philippa Vaughan (ed.), *The Victoria Memorial Hall Calcutta: Conceptions, Collections, Conservation* (Mumbai, 1997) cover the architecture of that remarkable building. For the Indo-Saracenic movement in general, see Christopher W. London (ed.), *Architecture in Victorian and Edwardian India* (Bombay, 1994). William Emerson's lecture 'On the Taj Mahal at Agra' was published in *Papers Read to the RIBA, 1869–70* (London, 1870). Edmund W. Smith's three major works are *The Moghul Architecture of Fathpur Sikri* (4 vols, Allahabad, 1894–8), *Moghul Decoration of Agra* (Allahabad, 1901) and *Akbar's Tomb, Sikandarah* (Allahabad, 1909). The most substantial work by Constance M. Villiers-Stuart is her *Gardens of the Great Mughals* (London, 1913).

CHAPTER 5

Lord Curzon's views on architecture and conservation in India are found scattered throughout his speeches, for which see Sir Thomas Raleigh (ed.), *Lord Curzon in India: Being a Selection from his Speeches ... 1898–1905* (London, 1906). See also Curzon's book, *British Government in India: The Story of the Viceroy's and Government Houses* (2 vols, London, 1925), which also includes his views on the Victoria Memorial Hall. Curzon's attitude to the Indian heritage is discussed by Derek Linstrum in the volume edited by Philippa Vaughan noted above and in an article titled 'The Sacred Past: Lord

Curzon and the Indian Monuments', in *South Asian Studies* (11, 1995).

Curzon's lamp is analysed by Thomas R. Metcalf in 'Past and Present: Towards an Aesthetic of Colonialism', in G. Tillotson (ed.), *Paradigms of Indian Architecture* (London, 1998). In alluding to Foucault and Said I have in mind works that have become primary texts for postcolonial critics, such as Michel Foucault, *L'Archéologie du savoir* (1969, translated as *The Archaeology of Knowledge*, London, 1972), and Edward Said, *Orientalism* (London, 1978) and *Culture and Imperialism* (London, 1993).

Details of the claims, counter claims, ill-considered projects and scams that are mentioned in this chapter are taken from the Indian press. An outline of the University of Illinois proposal for a 'Taj Mahal Cultural Heritage District' has been published by a team member, Amita Sinha, in *Architecture + Design* (20/6, 2003). *Bunty aur Babli* is available on DVD from Yash Raj Films and is highly recommended.

ACKNOWLEDGEMENTS

I am grateful to Mary Beard and Peter Carson for inviting me to contribute this crucial volume to Profile Books' 'Wonders of the World' series, and for their candid and constructive editorial comments and suggestions. I am also indebted to David Watkin (many years ago my Director of Studies in Cambridge), who might have written this book himself but who, with characteristic generosity, recommended a former student in his place. I thank the two anonymous readers for the Harvard University Press edition for their corrections and many helpful suggestions. For moral support and generous help I thank Mitch Crites, Andrew Franklin, Niall Hobhouse, Sunil Khilnani, Ajit Ninan, Alison Ohta, Sharmila Sen, Ranjana Sengupta, Jug Suraiya and Nicola Taplin.

In studying the Taj Mahal I have learnt much from leading specialists in the field of Mughal architecture, and particularly from Ebba Koch, Wayne Begley, Z. A. Desai, Catherine Asher and Elizabeth Moynihan, as readers of their books will readily detect. I cannot expect them to approve of all of my arguments but I hope that they will find them stimulating.

Closer to home, I owe most to Vibhuti, who did double duty on holding the baby and who still found time to read and comment on the manuscript.

LIST OF ILLUSTRATIONS

INDEX

WONDERS OF THE WORLD

This is a small series of books that will focus on some of the world's most famous sites or monuments. Their names will be familiar to almost everyone: they have achieved iconic stature and are loaded with a fair amount of mythological baggage. These monuments have been the subject of many books over the centuries, but our aim, through the skill and stature of the writers, is to get something much more enlightening, stimulating, even controversial, than straightforward histories or guides. The series is under the general editorship of Mary Beard. Other titles in the series are: